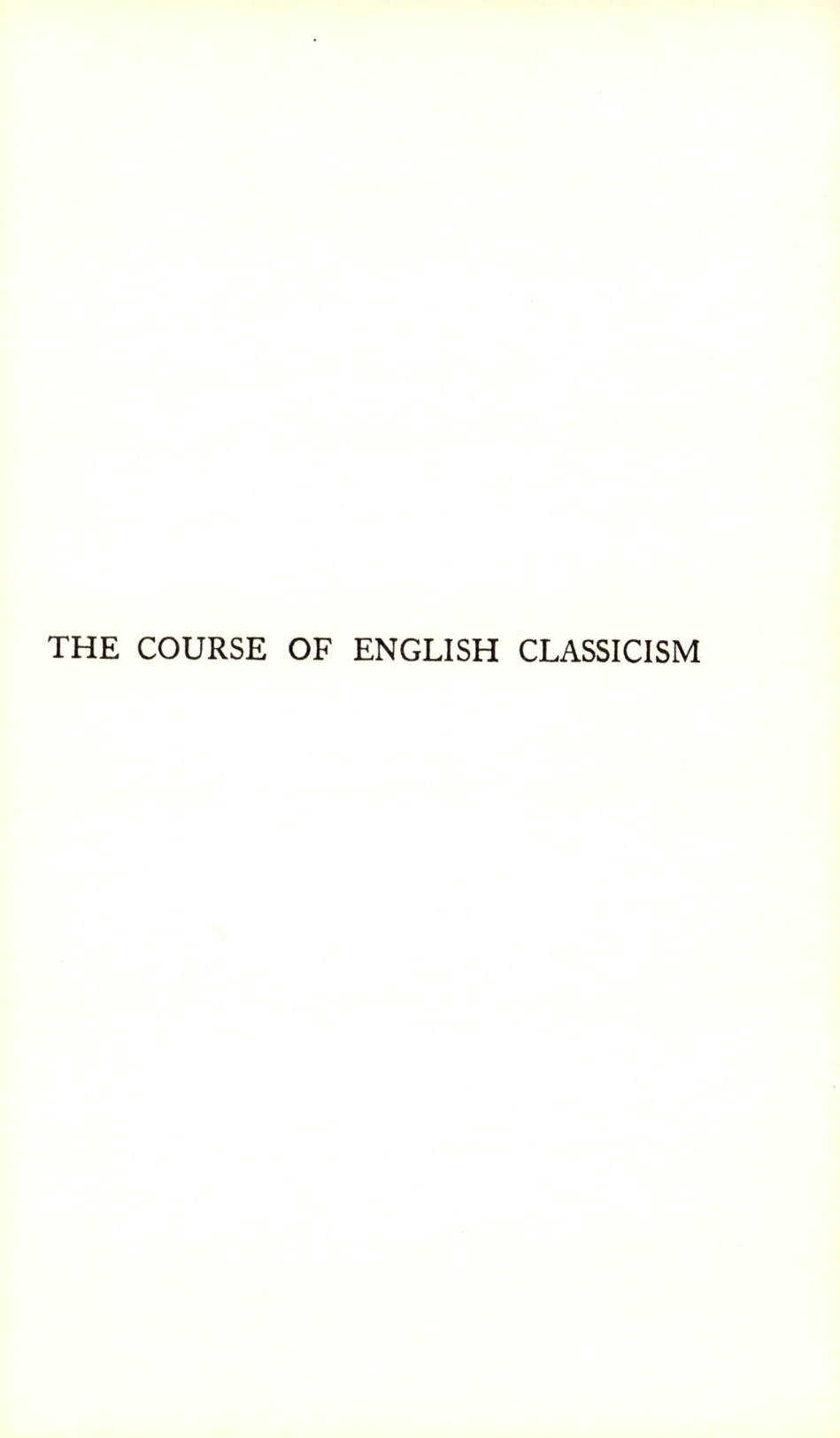

THE COURSE OF ENGLISH CLASSICISM

THE COURSE OF ENGLISH CLASSICISM

FROM THE TUDOR TO THE VICTORIAN AGE

SHERARD VINES

Phaeton Press

New York

1968

ORIGINALLY PUBLISHED 1930
REPRINTED 1969

PUBLISHED BY PHAETON PRESS, INC.
Library of Congress Catalog Card Number 70-91351

CONTENTS

		PAGE
I.	THE BEGINNINGS	7
II.	THE RISE OF THEORY	32
III.	NATURE METHODISED	45
IV.	THE AGE OF BAROQUE AND THE GRAND MANNER	61
V.	POLITENESS AND GOOD SENSE	76
VI.	GEORGIAN DEVELOPMENTS	109
VII.	THE LATER CLASSICISM	133
	INDEX	158

A COURSE OF ENGLISH CLASSICISM

CHAPTER I

THE BEGINNINGS

" At length Erasmus, that great injur'd name
(The glory of the Priesthood, and the shame !)
Stemm'd the wild torrent of a barbarous age
And drove those holy Vandals off the stage."
POPE, *Essay on Criticism*.

BEFORE Henry VIII's accession, events preliminary to our study were taking place. Erasmus first visited England in 1499, when Henry VII had been on the throne, and Malory's *Morte Arthur* in circulation, for fourteen years. Tudor Humanism was by this time gathering force : scholars such as More, Colet, Grocyn, or Linacre became active : and Erasmus expressed in a letter his admiration of the abundance of the harvest of learning in this country. In purely native work, like *Fulgens and Lucres*, we can discern the newer spirit fighting to subdue, or at least express itself adequately through, the older form. The desire for a politer art was there, and with foreign aid it began to find utterance in several departments. Torrigiano came to the help of architecture before 1512 : Jan Gossaert, followed in 1526 by Holbein, laid a foundation, tardily built upon, for a saner pictorial art. Barclay, following Mantuan, began to pave the way for *The Shepheard's Kalender*, and Skelton, whom Erasmus described to Henry VIII as " Britannicarum literarum decus et lumen," was a grammarian, an accomplished Latin scholar, and tilted, as we know from *Speke Parrot*, at unsatisfactory methods of teaching Greek at Universities :

" But our Grekis, their Greke so wel have applied
That they cannot say in Greke, riding by the way
' Now hosteler, fetche my horse a bottel of hay.' "

Skelton, like Shakespeare after him, was offended by the pedantry which, as M. Anatole France reminded us,[1] was not a new parasite confined to the Renaissance, but bred in the old scholasticism. His own poetry is not governed by the law and order which was coming out of Italy : grotesque and flamboyant Gothic predominates, and *The Tunnyng of Eleanour Rummyng* is the direct descendant of the carouse in *Piers Plowman*. It is significant that Gothic buildings, and good Gothic at that, continued to go up during the sixteenth century : King's College chapel at Cambridge was only begun a few years before Torrigiano came ; and that plays of a medieval type were to

[1] Cf. M. France's lectures on Rabelais (recently translated into English).

remain in favour for many a day as yet, although a change from scriptural subjects to dramatisations of scholarly and even scientific notions marks the course of a slow and difficult transformation. The struggle between the Gothic and popular art, and the more aristocratic art assisted by the importation and Royal patronage of foreigners, or again, by Italianisers like Wyatt and Surrey,—and of the doctrine or faith behind those arts, was still bitter in Elizabeth's day. The conflict in *Dr. Faustus* is to a large extent one between classic scepticism and Gothic belief ; Faustus, personifying the spirit of intellectual curiosity and observation which implies the sceptical attitude ; personifying that spirit in Marlowe and his age, and attempting to free himself from that medieval damnation and salvation, which still obsessed more minds than the poet's, is yet unable to do so, and is damned ; the old tradition is too strong for him.

Rewards and fairies, if not eternal punishments, did, however, gradually recede into corners where enlightened Protestantism could not easily get at them ; yet it was not till Corbet's time that they were lamented in set terms, though Milton kept them alive for decorative purposes between the days of Drayton and Dryden's " fairy way of writing." It would be a mistake to call Protestantism a necessary part of the *Classical* Renaissance in England. More, one of the first and foremost humanists, was a Catholic, and Puritanism, that

Protestant extreme, battled against art, from Gosson until the closing of the theatres, and even later.

Much of the Tudor period was given to absorption of and exercise in fresh ideas. When Surrey and Wyatt attempted the Italian style of versification, English poetry was scarcely prepared for it, as one may well imagine ; the fourteener and Poulter's measure (the fourteener is merely a ballad measure undivided) stubbornly held their own. Petrarch, the model for the new poetic school, used alliteration to some extent, but the ponderous alliteration of Tudor verse before Spenser is far more in keeping with the Saxon precedent of *Piers Plowman* and other poems of that time. Barnabe Googe's eclogues bear everywhere the footprints of the rude swain ; Lord Vaux, Churchyard, and even Gascoigne could tramp heavily along with awkward strides.

> " My glancing lookes are gone, which wonted were to prie
> On everie gorgious garishe glasse, that glistred in mine eie,"

while Turbervile makes the coarsest homespun out of classic elegance :

> " And if Admetus' darling deare were of so fresh a face
> Though Phœbus kept Admetus' flock it may not him disgrace."

But when he thus addresses Neptune, " O Neptune, churlish chuf, O wayward woolf," he is not far off from the wild, though later, barbarisms of Stanyhurst's *First Foure Books of Virgil his Aeneis*,[1] from which Nashe quotes with dismay:

" Then did he make heavens vault to rebound, with rounce robble hobble
Of ruffe raffe roaring, with thwick thwack thurlery bouncing."

This is perhaps the most unclassical englishing of a classic that we have; he might well have been whipt for o'erdoing Termagant. That such a portent should occur so late in the century goes to prove that classic decorum had a long fight of it before its law and order could be imposed, and that what the humanists had sown under Henry VIII was no more than sprouting under Elizabeth. The combination of ferocious heartiness with the new culture was seen at its best in Rabelais; of whom we might never have had adequate translations had the heartiness not lingered on through the next century, with Urquhart (d. 1660), and Motteux (d. 1718).

[1] Book I opens thus:
" I that in old season wyth reeds oten harmonye whistled
My rural sonnet: from forrest flitted (I) forced
Thee sulcking swincker thee soyle, thoghe craggie, to sunder.
A labor and a trauaile to plowswayns hertelye welcoom
Now manhood and garbroyls I chaunt and martial horror . . ."
Which is mild in comparison with the amazing stuff that follows. Thus, of Mercury's rod he writes:
". . . by which from the helly Bocardo
Touzt tost souls he freeth. . . ." (ARBER's ed.).

In the earlier part of the sixteenth century Roger Ascham (1515-68) made the first serious effort at English criticism, if he did not succeed in disentangling the issues of art from those of morals. He judged the fitness of Sallust as a subject for study not only by the roughness of his style, but by his having "spent the most part of his youth very misorderly in ryot and lechery," and censured romance on purely ethical grounds, since the whole pleasure of *Morte Arthur* "standeth in . . . open man's slaughter and bold bawdrye." Yet he laid a solid part of the foundations of English classicism, as one writing English to Englishmen—for so he styles himself. He knows the great worth of discipline by rule, and has no approval for those who say "it were a plaine slaverie, and injurie to, to shakkle and tye a good wit . . . with such bondes of servitude." On views such as these depends much that went to the making of Augustanism : and there occurs beside in Ascham reference to the gods of Augustan æsthetic. He makes several allusions to Horace and one to Aristotle's *Poetics* which, Professor Gregory Smith points out, is probably the first of its kind ; and these two authorities were made responsible for a very great deal—some of which might have surprised them—in the next century. Horace was already enthroned, and in Elizabeth's age extended his dominion not only over noble scholars like Sidney, but over such pseudo-classicists as Webbe, who could end an English Sapphic stanza with "thou art down in a dump dasht!" (*Of English Poetry*, 1586.)

The Scholemaster, read as a whole, is sufficient evidence that Ascham was no pedant ; yet he fell into the error whereto Gabriel Harvey tried to convert Spenser, the belief that rhyme was barbarous and that English versification should set before itself the ideal of the dactylic hexameter : and the couplet of Watson's that he sets forth "for an Example to good wittes" merely helps to demonstrate how little as yet the spirit of classicism had really penetrated and united with the English genius :

" All travellers do gladly report great praise of Ulysses
   For that he knew many men's maners, and saw many
      cities."

All that we can say of this is that it is better than Gabriel Harvey's[1] absurdities : the distich on the laurel is well known :

"What might I call this tree ? A laurell ? O bonny
   Laurell,
Needes to thy bowes will I bow this knee, and vaile my
   bonctto."

Upon ineptitudes like this Nashe leapt with a justifiably savage delight when he took off poor Gabriel :

[1] 1545-1630.

"But ah! What newes have you heard of that good
    Gabriel huff snuff,
 Known to the world for a fool, and clapt in the Fleet for
    a rymer."

What Ascham felt was largely true—that the poets of his time, with their clod-hopping Poulter's measure cut a very poor figure beside Homer or Horace, and that Norton, and even Wyatt and Surrey, fell short of the mark of elegance.

That imitation of the Ancients which he recommends was at this phase of the Renaissance a necessary exercise for the assimilation of that polite form that should preclude "a devorse betwixt the tong and the hart." And there was more to be assimilated than the mere outward form. "The order and doctrine of *Imitation* would bring forth more learning and breed up truer judgment, than any other exercise that can be used." Had this precept been more universally followed the Harveys and Stanyhursts of a later age (though Stanyhurst boldly refers to him) would have used greater discretion.

Ascham was not alone in his campaign for sanity: he confesses a debt, in displaying the instruments of Imitation, to his friend Sir John Cheke (1514-57); and Sir Thomas Wilson in his *Arte of Rhetoric* (1553) was busy defending England from pedantries and preciosities, such as the young men brought back from their Italian tour,—a mode of "finishing" that Ascham deprecates:

or forced into the language by false scholars of the type of Rabelais' young Limousin student. These gentry were still at work in Shakespeare's day, and he gives us samples of them in Holofernes and Sir Nathaniel. But though the more infectious preciosity of euphuism was to win back some of the ground that Ascham and his peers had gained for a noble English prose, the reverse was not decisive, and before Lyly's death (1606) the advance toward the grand manner had been resumed. Euphuism was a curious flower of a youthful season in the Renaissance, at which the decorative possibilities of a great wealth of material were being recognised and exploited, before a maturer judgment learnt to cut out the superfluous and trust for effect not so much in the particulars of adornment as in the general effect of the whole and the relation to it of its parts.

The balance of a Latin sentence, whether in Cicero or Seneca, was by this time appreciated by English authors; but the piling up of sentences balanced by parallelism or antithesis in Lyly's *Euphues* (1578) suggests that then the larger view of form had yet to be appreciated. *Euphues* is little more than a heap of jewels. A decorative sense of this order might be expected during the fusion of a stiff and highly ornate but living Gothic tradition with the Græco-Roman ideal; and some of the ornaments themselves, such as the allusions to natural history, though they are drawn largely from Pliny, would tickle the ears of those who knew the zoology of medieval bestiaries or Mandeville. The refinements of euphuism owed something to those of Italy and Spain; Guevara's "lofty style" in his book which North translated as *The Diall of Princes* certainly affected Lyly; but Lyly's style, and his imitators', was made natural to the soil, and an organic part of English culture. The ornament, the forced balance, and the grotesque combine to render in words the effect given on copper by such engravings as those of Étienne Delaune (1519–83) in which an inspiration still partly Gothic seeks to express itself in a Renaissance mode.

What Euphuism and cognate tendencies to preciosity achieved was an attempt at refinement and the promotion of not merely verbal but intellectual play; and Shakespeare, who certainly studied Lyly with care, was a master at this game of ideas which he redeemed from its grosser affectations. For these, indeed, he felt contempt, and managed to caricature the various Elizabethan crotchets both early and late, in *Love's Labour's Lost* and in *King Lear*. But this contempt burnt brightly only at moments when he was especially aware of a barbaric absurdity; as when Rombus of the *Arcadia* or the pedant Josse of Larivey's *Le Fidelle* (as interpreted by Munday) may have set him on the track of some queer characters whom he had met. But when nothing has stimulated this awareness, we may judge him to have been witty after the new fashion, without satirical intent, and without dreaming that he was otherwise than elegant, as the usage then was, with his puns and conceits. The pun on " case " that Lear lets off on poor blind Gloucester seemed to Shakespeare, no doubt, to be in the best of taste.

He was not the only one to see the dangers of false scholarship and eccentricity, nor the only one to be affected by such things himself. Thomas Nashe had a keener detective sense for what was unseemly or unbalanced, but his own eagerness and exuberance sometimes betrayed him. He could smell out " the ingrafted overflow of some kilcow conceipt " and yet give us an astounding euphuistic reference to the panther's degenerate taste ; in spite of which he was still able to say of *Euphues,* which he read when " a little ape at Cambridge," " to imitate it I abhorre, otherwise than it imitates Plutarch, Ovid, and the choicest Latine Authors." Perhaps he would have called in Pliny to defend his panther. He was right in attacking " Seneca let bloud line by line," and the more Senecan bursts of Kyd, as he does in the preface to *Menaphon* (1589). In the same work he finds that Stanyhurst, that " Thrasonicall huffe snuffe," " trod a foule, lumbering, boystrous, wallowing measure in his translation of Vergil." He knew well enough that the true humanists had the better manners, that Erasmus, More, Cheke, and Ascham were the kind that "repurged the errors of Arts expelde from their puritie" but, living himself in an air infected with semi-Gothic impurities, he must in some degree fall sick of the malady.

His disapproval of Romance is based on more strictly literary grounds than Ascham's; the "scamblyng shift" in *Bevis of Hamptoun* to find rhymes offends him, as do "the fantasticall dreames of those exiled Abbie-lubbers from whose idle pens proceeded worne-out impressions of the feyned nowhere acts of Arthur . . . Sir Tristram, Hewon of Bordeaux. . . ." and so forth. This blow is aimed very definitely at the Gothic; and what Nashe wished to substitute for these thread-bare fables was a more decorous humanity—the Fountains of Truth rather than the Rivers of Opinion. This was why he grew impatient with those who loitered by the way, made "toyes their onlie studie," and would "excruciate themselves about impertinent questions as . . . whether *Achilles* or *Patroclus* were older" or "in what Moneth of the yere *Virgill* died." He is groping for the classic principle which we shall meet again and again hereafter, that what is more general is our first consideration, and that there is a danger of getting lost among details and particulars. Elizabethan prose style came through this peril, not indeed unscathed, because there were men, like Nashe, with the larger view.

Lodge and Greene both followed Lyly's euphuistic lead; and Gabriel Harvey, who had his own æsthetic idiosyncrasies, found himself opposed on personal grounds to Greene, and then Nashe, who took up the cudgels against Gabriel Huffe Snuffe at a later stage. Gabriel, no good judge of what is seemly, speaks admiringly and in the same breath of Stanyhurst and Sidney because they took a hint from his theory of classical metres. But he was not altogether either fool or pedant, and could write sanely enough about the over-decorated stuff, disguised Gothic-Arabesque, that was still admired by clever coteries. "Right artificiality ... is not mad-brained, or ridiculous, or absurd ... but pleasurable, but delicate, but exquisite, but gratious, but admirable; not according to the fantasticall mould of Aretine or Rabelais, but according to the fine modell of Orpheus, Homer, Pindarus, the excellentest wittes of Greece." By the way, there was more than a touch of Rabelaisian " heartiness" about Nashe's controversial style.

The truth was, of course, that all the various Elizabethan "artificialities" suffered in practice from mannerisms and an unrestfulness that betokened the youth of the age; Lyly, Harvey, Greene, Nashe, and Sidney, each in his own way strove to imitate the ancients, or Italian or Spanish imitators of them; but what they produced was nearer to classic art than Norman churches were to Roman basilicas—that and no more.

It was among such enthusiasts that the question of latinising English prosody was fought out. Harvey was in a conspiracy with Spenser for trying unsuccessfully the dactylic hexameter, but fortunately the experiments did not proceed very far. The discussion, and especially the part relating to rhyme or no rhyme, was taken into the next century by Campion and Daniel. Campion (*On English Verse*, 1602) brings up the usual argument that to rhyme is not to imitate the ancients, but to be barbarous; and he puts in a word against the excessive practice of alliteration which was, however, already doomed. He wisely rejected the dactyle, attempted lately "with passing pitifull success," and suggests modifications of Latin forms, some of which, like his dimeter and Anacreontic, remain with us, rhymed or further modified; while his

> "Rose-cheekt *Laura*, come
> Sing thou smoothly with thy beawtie's
> Silent musicke, either other
> Sweetely gracing,"

survives as a moving poem rather than as an example of "rational" Sapphic.

Daniel replied in the next year, defending rhyme; and amongst other valuable things he says, in effect that, the true spirit of culture is not seen in a mere parade of "Anapestiques, Trochies, and Tribracques," of which the civilised Chinese are ignorant. He can thus bring himself into opposition to current enthusiasm for the Renaissance ; if the Tudor age brought us Erasmus and More, he declares (like some of our moderns), the Middle Ages gave us St. Thomas and Duns Scotus. His defence of rhyme was vindicated in the most classical age of Dryden when, curiously enough, the opinions he set forth as a concession to the anti-rhyming party were reversed, viz., that the rhymed couplet can be very tiresome and unpleasing, and that blank verse (which was the convention of the Senecan dramatists) was appropriate to tragedy. Daniel was inclined to take a large view, and to see that the question of rhyme or no rhyme had not the greatest importance in " that perpetuall revolution which we see to be in all things that never remaine the same, and we must heerein be content to submit our selves to the law of time, which in few yeeres wil make al that for which we now contend *Nothing*."

The " will to classicism," if it had imposing obstacles to surmount, grew steadily in vigour, and laboured with such persistence that before the century closed England was becoming fairly impregnated—the process went further perhaps than one may suspect—by the new humanities. Pistol and his comrades were echoing at second-hand the mouth-filling tragic stuff of Seneca, and we may well believe, that some at least of the village yokels had heard of Phibbus' car and Ninny's tomb from their parson and schoolmaster ; Smug in *The Merrie Devil of Edmonton* (soon after 1600) mentions "the goddesses and the destinies" to the priest, Sir John. Shop assistants and ladies' maids were still reading the old romances; but some rumours of the new fiction may well have reached them.

This dealt with more than *Euphues*, and took on a colouring from the late Greek authors, Achilles Tatius and his like. The translators were busy, and exercised in general greater judgment than Stanyhurst, though more cannot be said. Phaer's earlier Virgil was rude, Golding (1565), Turbervile and others rendered Ovid in verse of varying merit. Drant translated the *Satires* and *Epistles* of Horace, and Chapman's *Iliad* crowned this industry in 1598. His Homer is not a thing to be sneered at; both the *Iliads* and the *Odysseys* are turned by him into undeniable English poetry, unexpectedly alive and solid. Chapman is a Triton among the minors; he has solved the problem, insoluble for most Elizabethans, of achieving vigour without eccentricity, so little of which is to be found here that we are almost shocked at "the horrid tennis" of Eurus and Zephyr. The *Iliad* in fourteeners does not succeed as splendidly as the *Odyssey*, where Chapman shows us, as he does in that double flower of the Renaissance, *Hero and Leander*, his mastery of the run-on heroic couplet. The music is harsh beside Pope's—how indeed should it be otherwise? It moves with a masculine, bearded dignity that was before the time of periwigs:

> " Together all this time Jove's thunder chid,
>   And through and through the ship his lightning glid
>   Till it embrac'd her round : her bulk was fill'd
>   With nasty sulphur, and her men were kill'd,
>   Tumbled to sea, like sea-mews swum about
>   And there the date of their return was out."

It was regrettable though inevitable that some Greek and Latin literature would have come to the translators at second hand, and that certain inferior works (Seneca's theatre was in its time only less crucial than the Laocoön was many years after), becoming known before the better, should have given a definite twist to our nascent culture. Gascoigne's and Kinwelmershe's *Jocasta* (1566) was based on the Italian of Dolce which in turn had been drawn from Euripides' *Phœnissæ* ; Underdowne went to the Latin of a Pole, one Warschewiczki for his Heliodorus' *Æthiopica*, while North's Plutarch owed much to the Frenchman Amyot.

The influence of the Greek novelists has been traced in Lyly, and faintly in Lodge. Greene was certainly affected by Achilles Tatius, Heliodorus, and Longus, upon whom he drew for ornament ; but Sidney makes the largest use of these romances in his *Arcadia*. There are certain well-known episodes and situations which have their sources in Greek fiction ; the pastoral element of Greene's *Pandosto* has some echoes from *Daphnis and Chloe*, and from the *Æthiopica* comes that shipwreck tale which became at length the well-known disaster off the Bohemian coast. Sidney borrows pirate-episodes from Achilles Tatius, and uses three times in *Arcadia* the devices of a pretended execution that occurs twice in *Clitophon and Leucippe*. Such adventures and perils are typical of the Greek writers; but other sorts of adventure, coming from Spain with *The Pleasant Historie of Lazarillo de Tormes*, fulfilled a "lower" function in meeting a demand for the life of the submerged and for picaresque wanderings of rogues. Nash's *Unfortunate Traveller* supplied also such a demand, which the loftier kind of fiction, *Rosalynde* or *Euphues* or the *Arcadia*, evidently failed to satisfy.

Though Greene and Sidney derived some pastoral *décor* from the Greeks, there were other sources for the establishment of this delicious convention; the Spaniard Montemayor, whose *Diana* appeared in 1552 inspired Googe, Sidney, and Spenser; and the *Arcadia* was in some measure indebted to the *Arcadia* of Sanazzaro (1504). Lodge, we recollect, took more than a hint from Sidney for his own *Rosalynde*. Barclay (1475–1552) had followed the Latin eclogues of the Italian Mantuan, though he was acquainted with Virgil; but Mantuan was more familiar in England as a school textbook. Once more, Spenser, in the *Shepheard's Kalender*, openly declared his debt to Marot. These are but selected instances of the manner in which our English Arcadia began to grow out of derived classic beginnings, till it became a garden for poets and dramatists, for Browne of Tavistock, Milton, Aurelian Townshend, or Pope himself, to beautify in succeeding generations.

On the stage Plautus and Terence formed a not too distant background for comedy, while tragedy began to assume a more classic shape from Seneca and his disciple Garnier. Nicholas Udall (1505–56) bequeathed to us the Plautine figure of Roister Doister, since when the type of the *miles gloriosus* has appeared in various disguises, as Pistol, as Braggadochio, as Bobadil, as Shadwell's Captain Hackum.[1] The nurse type, another recurrent, comes to us through Italian comedies based on Terence and Plautus; such is Balia of Gascoigne's *Supposes*, translated from Ariosto and produced in 1566. This nurse is a refinement on the bawd or *lena* of Latin comedy, but retains something of the nature of a mercenary go-between, and as such passes into *Romeo and Juliet*, *Two Gentlemen of Verona*, and other plays. Of the pert servants, valets, and soubrettes whose importance increased as Renaissance comedy developed, there are early examples in Squartacantino of *The Buggbeares*, and the *ancilla* of *Menæchmi* which Warner englished in 1595. Larivey (1540–1611), a French Plautine comedy writer who derived his matter from the Italian, was another foreign source and intermediary, and dealt in impudent lacqueys and servant

[1] In *The Squire of Alsatia*.

girls as well as in pedants ; but one may bear in mind that the *ancilla* was made known on the stage by Medwall as early as 1497 or thereabouts.

But, if classical drama called attention to " life below stairs," it was not very long before this life and character was being refashioned upon English models. Ben Jonson, who, incidentally, owned a fifteenth-century manuscript of Terence, went to Plautus for *The Case is Altered*, found Strobilus the slave in *Aulularia*,—a creature compounded of naïve cunning and complacency, but proceeded to anglicise the type in Onion and Juniper. Again, that brazen hussy, pretty Mistress Wagtail, from Field's *A Woman is a Weathercock* (1609) is entirely English and has read *Bevis of Hamptoun*.

The great Greek masters of tragedy being practically unknown in Elizabethan England, Seneca had it all his own way. Soon after 1550 his tragedies, or copies of them, were being acted in Latin at the Universities ; and in 1561 *Gorboduc*, a drama of " The matter of Britain," but in the Senecan manner, by Sackville and Norton, was performed at the Inner Temple, to be followed by Gascoigne's *Jocasta* at Gray's Inn in 1566. The Latin plays continued in colleges, but were now rivalled by English tragedies in the classical style like Legge's *True Tragedie of Richard II* (1579),[1] the precursor of Shakespeare's History.

[1] *Seneca His Ten Tragedies* (1581) was a translation by Newton.

The modern contempt of *Gorboduc* has been overdone : and the present writer can testify that an amateur performance of it impressed with dignity and gravity an audience fortunately unschooled to deride everything Senecan.

Medieval drama, though in its dotage, was meanwhile attempting to survive in a thin classic disguise ; the "tyrant's vein" of *King Cambises* was interpreted on the boards in 1569, after *Jocasta*. But the pseudo-classic interlude, which, as *Fulgens and Lucres* will bear witness, had once promised well, was now doomed, though before it died it had disturbed the classical conventions of the drama sufficiently to allow full freedom for Shakespeare, who broke other things beside the Unities. Yet indeed, even if there had not been the excuse of that mad lad the Vice for the antics and liberties of mature Elizabethan drama, some other would have been found for so flamboyant a phase. As for ramping and roaring in the style of Herod, the Senecan drama as followed in *Gismond of Salerne* (1567–8) and *The Misfortunes of Arthur* (1588) or by Garnier and his disciple Kyd, gave ample opportunity for this. Seneca himself can "quail, crash, conclude, and quell" in this manner (Deianira in *Hercules Œtæus*) :

> "Utinam esset, utinam fixus in Thalamis meis
> Herculeus ensis ! Huic decet ferro immori
> Una perire dextera nobis sat est ?
> Coite, gentes, saxa et immensas faces
> jaculetur orbis. . . ."

Garnier is equally violent in passion; his Cornelia, and Kyd's, lament without action or intermission through five acts: and Guinevere is sometimes as noisy on the stage as Cornelia. But in Kyd's original work and where his model is concealed by other elements, as in *The Spanish Tragedy*, the solemn march of the classic pentameter is checked by prose passages; action increases, and poetry in the romantic vein appears:

" My hart (sweet frend) is like a ship at sea;
   She wisheth port, where riding all at ease
   She may repaire what stormie times have worne,
   And leaning on the shore may sing with joy (etc.)."

And we thus pass to the next stage in which, upon a Senecan foundation, romantic drama is built to culminate in Shakespeare. There remain the ghosts, descendants of Tantalus' ghost in *Thyestes*, the tragedy of blood, and to some extent that of revenge; the chorus soon disappears, but the convention of five acts (which Horace advised, and in which the form of *Gorboduc* had been cast according to Seneca's use) persists. But the Unities collapsed, and comic relief, that necessary condiment of the old sacred drama, established itself comfortably. *Hamlet* is a revenge drama based, if one may accept Mr. Boas' cogent argument, on an earlier play by the Senecan Kyd. It offends the Unities; it is well relieved with jesting and clowning, it presents a hero who, however you test him, emerges as a romantic. He has the high-falutin' style, the tendency to "fly away into the circumambient gas" that Mr. T. E. Hulme noted ; it is not merely that he would drink eisel, eat a crocodile, make Ossa like a wart, and otherwise behave unclassically. He passes beyond the human limit, the reasonable finiteness of man which is, in classicism, a limit set by and depending on sense—the Addisonian good sense. There are two kinds of elevation ; the romantic kind of that self-expansion in fantasy with which Hamlet consoles himself for inaction, like John-a-dreams unpregnant of his cause ; the " to be or not to be " passage is just this. Lear's madness is a similar compensation ; he imagines, in fantasy, that he is judging Goneril whom he is unable to judge in reality. It is an inward elevation, as opposed to the outward elevation achieved by reasoned enlargement of everything to scale, in the heroic plays of Dryden—the classic type. Nevertheless Mr. Hulme would claim Shakespeare for the Classics, and quoted in support the lines,

> " Golden lads and lasses must
> Like chimney-sweepers, come to dust."

The word " lads," he maintained, is classical : but the romantic if perhaps slightly mistaken admirers and imitators of *The Shropshire Lad* evidently do not think so. He continues to the effect that modern romantics would have written "youth." Surely not; the term "youth" is more general than "lad," and therefore more in accordance with the poetic practice of neo-classicism. "The generous youth forgets his crown," sang Lloyd in his entirely classical *Arcadia* (1760). Cowley had cried "ah, wretched youth!" before him, and Pope's Sappho addressed Phaon as "lovely youth": the word fairly reeks of Augustanism, of all that is repugnant to romantics. There is, it is true, a thin classic veneer over much of Shakespeare's work; the inevitable decoration from the old mythologies is there, if in no great profusion. *Richard III* has been called his most Senecan play; again, there are his experiments with the chorus, and there is more than one ghost. All of which features do not necessarily make a classic author, and in this instance, certainly not.

Other tests may be applied; he has, as Malory had, that gift of suggestion, of "incantation" when dealing with landscape, that is essentially romantic. Neither describe minutely or at length; one samphire-gatherer leaves a heap of detail to be added; yet we feel a wildness, a glamour about the scenery in *Morte Arthur* or, let us say, in *Cymbeline* or *The Tempest*, that we do not in Denham's *Cooper's Hill* or Pope's *Windsor Forest*. There is a difference between this method and the more "particular" method of modern romantics, the discussion of which does not come within the purview of this book.

The thrill is not merely confined to the subject of landscape; we find it in the sonnets, in *Antony and Cleopatra*, but not in Waller or Herrick or for that matter in Horace or *Les Chansons de Bilitis*. This magic, this use of words to play havoc in direct assault upon our senses, is the method of romanticism; if not, what can be called romantic? We cannot impose such arbitrary limitations on the term.

Mr. Hulme discerned two kinds of classicism, the static and the dynamic. This is correct; but to call Shakespeare a dynamic classic is not; he is dynamic, but not classic. Dynamic classicism is Baroque, the Baroque of Dryden, Vanbrugh, or Salvator, which must be distinguished from romantic content overlaid with classic decoration and cast in more or less classic form, that characterises so much Elizabethan work. Professor Bosanquet observed, very truly, that "Sidney, Corneille, Shaftesbury as an art critic, Lord Kaimes, Batteux, Lessing, were all interested ... in the adjustment of modern æsthetic feeling, always comparatively speaking romantic, to the classical tradition." Sidney went further in theory than many writers before Jonson succeeded in doing, in practice: but after Jonson, whom Professor Bosanquet might have included in his list, there was more evidence that both form and content, if this duality can be admitted, deviated further from the romantic path.

CHAPTER II

THE RISE OF THEORY

AFTER giving Ascham his due, we may say that English Æsthetic is not much older than news of the Armada. Stephen Gosson, when he hoisted his puritanical "Flagge of Defiance," had merely stimulated Sidney to pass from the "moral-æsthetic" to the clearer vision, and refer to Horace and Aristotle. He established principles which remained henceforth in the classic apparatus of criticism, and emphasised others that, like the rules of dramatic construction, still required encouragement; his whole trend being towards what is seemly, decorous, and noble. Through Aristotle he arrives at the general or universalising treatment of a subject by the artist (*Apologie for Poetrie*, 1583). Poetry is imitation, but it deals "with *Katholou* . . . the universall consideration; and the history with *Kathekaston*, the particuler."

His next step is clearly to argue "*ut poesis, pictura*"; the painter has the same selective rights as the poet; and so, if "nature never set forth the earth in so rich tapistry as the poets have done," the more excellent painters will show the outward beauty of a virtue in their portraits, i.e. will indicate a general abstract idea. From poetry of this kind we obtain delight and medicine ; he claims, indeed, though in more " emotive " terms, that poetry is capable of doing for the reader quite as much as the " pseudo-statement " of Mr. Richards.[1] In so doing he defends more than once that feature of the " age of reason " which we have forgotten how to enjoy—the didactic poem ; for did not Thales, Empedocles, and Parmenides sing their natural philosophy in verses ?

He views drama strictly, as Dryden views Ben Jonson. *Gorboduc* pleases him with its stately Senecan language, but offends through its failure to observe the Unities of place and time ; and " if it is so in *Gorboduc*, how much more in all the rest ? " The other anti-classical practice that comes up for censure before him and Dryden is " mingling kings and Clownes . . . (to) thrust in Clownes by head and shoulders, to play a part in majestical matters, with neither decencie or discretion." This feeling for decency and discretion sets him against flamboyance of the euphuistic sort, " a Curtizan-like painted affectation," the out-Cicero-ing of Cicero, the rifling-up of Herbarists and " Stories of Beastes, Foules, and Fishes." Sidney the critic and Sidney the Maker do not always see eye to eye. In the *Apologie* itself there is " the Hedghog that drave out the Vipers, that with their birth kill their parents " ; and the *Arcadia* betrays a high standard

[1] v. *Science and Poetry*.

of ornamental technique. But as a theorist he has moved strongly forward, away from Classicised Gothic toward a purer style. Spenser ennobled the former, and imparted to it a spaciousness that more than anything of the Euphuists', partakes of Renaissance dignity; his proportions, the breadth of his sweep, were anticipatory of those of the grand manner in the next century. To what he borrowed from Tasso he gave greater majesty, from Ariosto, an almost alien solemnity, as readers of *The Faërie Queene*, especially the last Canto of Book II, will no doubt agree. Fortified and disciplined by a wide learning, he imparted to English letters something of that order and decorum which the classic tradition intends: his wandering after Harvey's *ignis fatuus* into the slough of latinised " unhappie verses " and his graver lapse in the opposite direction of antique pastiche are easily forgiven for the sake of all the rest. But the pastiche was not so easily forgiven by Sidney and Ben Jonson, whose appreciation of what is controlled and reasonable drove them to deplore it. Sidney was more of a professional critic than Spenser, and was familiar with the classicist Aristotelian views of Italians like Scaliger, Minturno, or Castelvetro, who were writing poetic a little earlier in the century.

Ben Jonson, swearing allegiance to Horace and Aristotle, succeeded to the critic throne, from which he issued not merely edicts but examples.

"Poetry and picture," he wrote, "are arts of a like nature, and both busy about imitation," but " not to imitate servilely, as Horace saith, and catch at vices for virtue, but to draw forth out of the best and choicest flowers with the bee, and turn all into honey . . . make the imitation sweet." This is the classical or selective view of art, the headstone in the corner. But another basic demand is for forge and file, that comes from Horace's *Epistle to the Pisos*, which he translated :

> He'd bid blot all ; and to the Anvill bring
> Those ill-torn'd verses to new hammering.

Thus the " scabrous and rough " may be avoided ; and Jonson, if he did not always succeed in avoiding it as he was evidently so anxious to do, was a true controller of waywardness, as the remoteness of *Sejanus* from *The Revenger's Tragedy* may illustrate. *Rectitudo lucem fert : obliquitas et circumdatio offuscat* was a motto of his. His own taste, though it might be called silver rather than golden, impelled him along desirable paths. His famous and debated pronouncement that " Spenser, in affecting the ancients writ no language," is sound ; it means that he was alive to the dangers of pastiche, which was one of the very mainsprings of the romantic revival, and a formidable disturber of classic sobriety. As soon as the eighteenth century began to " think rude things greater than polished " a decadence was inevitable : the right Porphyrian tree fell sick ; the not wholly graceless Castle of Indolence was followed by the more gimcrack edifice of Otranto : fresh knights of the burning pestle, Chattertons and Macphersons, resumed that adventurous tone that had aroused Jacobean mirth, when those who were ignorant of Latin and Greek elegance yielded to the spell of romance. Yet, though the Porphyrian tree fell sick, there are signs that it has not been entirely destroyed, in spite of the Lyrical Ballads, of Ruskin's homilies, and more than a century of anarchic practice.

The humours of Jonson, and the Theophrastan characters of Earle, Hall, and Overbury fulfil another function in the development of classic art by preparing the way for the comedy of manners— of manners universal in or typical of species if not of genera. What lies behind humours and " characters," if some way behind them, is the Aristotelian ethical system : they are built up on the mean and on deviations from it ; and the deviations are not in the first instance particular idiosyncrasies but typical aberrations, the " melancholique " or the " phlegmatique." Overbury's " phantastique " young gallant is such a type widely distributed in literature (as late, indeed, as Dickens) and in life. " He accounts thoughtfulnesse as the wickedst thing in the world : and therefore studies impudence." Hall, " following that ancient Master of Morality," Theophrastus, starts, since " vertue is not loved enough," with types of the mean, the wise man, the humble man ; while his second book contains the deviations or " Characterismes of Vices," his preface to which suggests that he never loses sight of the abstract basis. Several times he begins a " character " (which might perhaps be called more aptly a " type ") with a definition of the quality that it impersonates.

The time was now coming when the antic, the curious conceit, was to pass with our metaphysical poets under the influence of a more complex and perhaps graver thought, and so become more organic ; when the " riche entayle " of a Rogers should give way to the severer methods of a Faithorne. And simultaneously, science was winning the first battles with superstition. It was in the seventeenth century that the philosopher appeared as something substantially more than a theologian, and much more than the " filosofre " of Chaucer ; and that a sort of nexus between art and philosophy, different from what is implied in Sidney's rather naïve claims, was possible. Bacon views art, in its widest sense, from a point of view which, if not strictly philosophical, is to some extent scientific. Art exists for him in any process whereby the constraint by man of nature for certain ends is achieved. " In things artificial nature seems as if it were made . . . a kind of second world." Arts are the bonds of nature ; but nature to be commanded must be obeyed, and man is her servant and interpreter (*Novum Organum*) ; nevertheless there is no doubt that Bacon believes in man's competence to assume command—yet let him not forget that the duty of his art is to perfect and exalt nature (*Advancement of Learning*). In interpreting the fable of Atalanta (*De Sapientia Veterum*) he makes it clear : " for Art, which is meant by Atalanta, is in itself, if nothing stand in the way, far swifter than Nature and, as one may say, the better runner, and comes sooner to the goal." His " art," then, includes the " knowledges and arts," mechanical skill and the methods of research being also concerned ; so that he is far from discussing unadulterated æsthetic.

Nevertheless, the principle of controlled nature here stated may surely be regarded as the precursor of the " Nature methodised " of Rapin and Pope, which long remained one of beauty's criteria. His jejune dicta on music and painting are scarcely helpful (*De Aug. Sci.*, IV. ii.) ; they are the highest of the voluptuary arts ; but of poesy he has more to say and, incidentally, of painting, in the *Advancement* (b. II). " Poetry is a part of learning in measure of words for the most part restrained, but in all other points extremely licensed, and doth truly refer to the imagination ; which, being not tied to the laws of matter, may at pleasure join that which nature hath severed, and sever that which nature hath joined, and so make unlawful matches and divorces of things : *pictoribus atque poetis* . . ."[1] In this way poetry is freer than history from close attention to individuals and particulars (*De Aug. Sci.*, II. i.); it can exceed the measure of nature and therefore approach nearer to universality, as art had actually done before the end of the century.

So liberated, poesy could portray " a more ample greatnesse, a more exact goodnesse, and a more absolute varietie than can be found in the Nature of Things. Therefore, because the Acts or Events of true Historie have not that Magnitude which satisfieth the minde of Man, poesie faineth Acts and Events Greater and More Heroicall." Thus, however much Bacon may elsewhere (to quote Bosanquet) have " championed the cause of particulars as if they were an oppressed population," he was laying down in this passage a foundation for the generalising style of his classic posterity, and for the grand manner, the heroic drama, the full sweep of Dryden, the boldness, and even the theatricality, of Baroque, though we may protest that many of these notions came from other and foreign sources, from Palladio and the French critics. But Aristotle

---

[1] The quotation from *Ars Poetica* continues:

"Quidlibet audendi semper fuit æqua potestas."

The authority for neo-classic practice qualifies this very strictly:

"Sed non ut placidis coeunt immitia, non ut
Serpentes avibus geminentur, tigribus agni."

But ideas of the seemly and the typical were not as yet deeply engrained in English poesy.

was already being studied in England from the Renaissance angle; he had remarked on the universality of poetry; and Bacon's foregoing observations may be read as a gloss on his pronouncement.

In passing let it be said that Bacon's taste for architecture when not governed by purely utilitarian motives, was of a kind that reflected the age, a kind less classical than that of Inigo Jones, the great English Palladian (1573–1652). Apart from Jones, indeed, there were practically no architects in the Elizabethan-Jacobean epoch whose conceptions were not either hampered by the Gothic usage or debased by German and Flemish influence. The master himself, in designing the scenery for Davenant's *Britannia Triumphans* twelve years after Bacon's death, saw no incongruity in a giant's castle with Gothic battlements and Renaissance windows, while the architecture of his setting for the City of Sleep in Davenant's *Luminalia* (1638) is similarly mixed.

Bacon would have cloisters and little turrets on the one hand, and " statuas " and a cupola on the other (*Essays*, XLV). The contemporary mixture of style is thus reflected—the taste of an age which had not forgotten the art of cusp and crocket. Bath Abbey was completed in 1616, in debased perpendicular, and Gothic-classic buildings went up, right through the century, at Oxford and elsewhere.[1]

[1] The Colleges of Jesus (1636), Lincoln (1631), and Brasenose (1666) are worth studying at Oxford, for architecture of this kind.

For Bacon, beauty is to be found in man rather than in his portrait; the best part of it is a "decent and gracious motion"; and he considers Dürer a trifler on what, to a modern critic, are frivolous grounds. He looks for that "which a picture cannot express" in man, and not in man's wild or picturesque setting of physical or geographical nature. The examination of that picturesque, which has been so conscientiously explored by Miss Manwaring and Mr. Hussey, developed at a later stage of classic evolution; but as long as it remained in classic bounds, so long did man continue to be the central, the dominant figure.

To discuss the beautiful in so many words was not Bacon's task, nor had he organised and consolidated his position in this section of knowledge; as it is, there seem to be left in detachment certain notions, such as that of a higher poesy "that would be thought to have in it something divine," and a lower, belonging to the voluptuary arts; and there is personal beauty, which "if it light well, it maketh virtue shine, and vices blush." But at least we have progressed thus far: to the view that poetry is an art of universals, that it is licensed to outrun nature, and that man is protagonist in the æsthetic comedy. These are recurrent threads in the history of classic art during the next century and a half, and more.

Hobbes, with his mechanic universe, has been recently attacked by no less a scholar than Mr. T. S.

Eliot[1] for an atheist and an emotive heretical corrupter of well-disposed (or neo-Thomist) minds. But nothing can lessen his importance as one who affected the drifts of thought both inside and outside philosophy ; and his view of the universe and of man's place in it, which gave a direction to subsequent ideas on poetic and allied theories, is not to be lightly dismissed. But first of all we may read, with profit and delight, his more exclusively literary essays. His reply to Davenant, which it is convenient to take before Davenant's own essay, shows him all for classic moderation and order, and carries us further than Bacon ; for whereas the latter granted unqualified licence to the imagination in poesy, the former imposes a limit ; there are to be no romantic embellishments, impenetrable armours, enchanted castles, and the like ; the beauty of a poem does not consist in the exorbitancy of its fiction. " For as truth is the bound of the Historical, so the resemblance of Truth is the utmost limit of Poeticall Liberty." One may compare his opinion on fancy (*The Virtues of an Heroic Poem*, 1675) ; " it flies," he writes, " swiftly to fetch in both matter and words ; but if there be not discretion at home to distinguish which are fit to be used and which not . . . their delight and grace is lost."

The artist, then, may exceed nature, but not the possibility of nature. An elephant must not be

[1] *For Lancelot Andrewes.*

painted two or three hundred miles long ; for expressionism he holds no brief, but on the contrary is leading toward the very wholesome doctrine of the type. His own preference is for a picture drawn " to the life," making " use of nothing but pure lines, without the help of any the least uncomely shadow."

Man is the central figure of his poetic ; it is not so much nature as " humane nature " that must be an author's theme and inspiration. " Valour, beauty, and love are his loftiest subjects; man is his proper study, while his design is not only to profit, but to delight the reader." Here is defined a sane humanism and a correlative demand for what Horace suggests as a worthy aim for poets :

" . . . simul et jucunda et idonea dicere vitæ."

In view of subsequent developments this seems to be a more important contribution to the treasury of criticism than his possibly better known distinction between judgment and wit or fancy, to which, nevertheless, a return will be necessary. Hobbes may have been, as Mr. Eliot claims, an emotionalist rather than a hard thinker ; but his mind had a desirable neatness ; he joins his art-theory to his universe with the links of time and memory, " the Mother of the Muses." Further, we may conclude that man's condition in his automatic system is not one of being resolved into the general flux of becoming lost in universal nature ; he is part of this nature, but a prominent and always integrated part. Herein, perhaps, lies the difference between the classic and the later views of his behaviour (man's, that is) ; in the latter he tends to disintegrate, to leave little but a few glands and reactions, in the way of manhood. The stress that Hobbes lays on the Intellectual Virtues (*Leviathan*, ch. viii) helps the reader to accompany him towards a humanised ideal which is in complete opposition to certain " dehumanising " tendencies in present-day thought ; and no one, surely, can come away from *The Leviathan* without some conviction that for Hobbes man, though he might be a member of the whole machine, was human, superior, and agreeing " by covenant only, which is Artificiall " (*Leviathan*, Pt. II, ch. xvi).

CHAPTER III
NATURE METHODISED

The importance of man, which no mechanic universe could materially lessen, is closely connected with the importance of the general in art and the methodising of nature ; man retained the right, throughout the neo-classic age, to select from and order nature for the purpose of art. " Imitate nature ! " was heard, it is true, on every side as criticism matured : " poesy," says Davenant (*Preface to Gondibert*, 1650), " is the best exposition of Nature " ; Horace, beside the warnings against unnatural extravagance at the outset, bids us—

" Aut famam sequere aut sibi convenientia fuge,"

while late in the history of artistic seemliness Goldsmith says that the author, in forming a character or describing a scene, must still keep nature in view " and refer every particular of his invention to her standard ; otherwise it will be a monster of incongruity " (*Essay* XIII, *Cultivation of Taste*).[1] But Rapin writing in 1672 holds that the rules of Horace and Aristotle demand that Nature should not be so much imitated as method-

[1] Mr. Blakeney, the scholarly editor of a recent edition of the *Ars Poetica*, calls attention to this passage in Goldsmith.

ised (*Réflexions sur la Poétique*), an idea which afterwards appealed to Pope. Dufresnoy's *De Arte Graphica* was published in 1668. It was the formulation of a creed which prevailed, or at least held, well into the nineteenth century. Which faith was this : that to paint universals was truly to paint nature, and that the genuine artist, neglecting particulars, should seek to give expression to his abstract ideals. Dufresnoy influenced many after Dryden ; and the importance and duration of his principles in precept, and practice such as Sir Joshua Reynolds's, is a sign that Schasler's view (cited by Bosanquet) that British æsthetic forsook Platonism in the eighteenth century, is wide of the mark. Mason brought out another translation in 1783 ; if there had been no demand for the book it would not have been worth publishing, but actually its influence is to be traced as far forward as Darley. Milton had already shown us the method, without the theory, in *L'Allegro* and *Il Penseroso*, two poems which influenced so profoundly the " landscape " school of eighteenth-century poets : Claude, who exhibited it on canvas, died in 1682, Gaspar Poussin in 1675, and Nicholas in 1665.

The English classic school of landscape painting, Wilson,[1] the Smiths of Chichester, Barret, laboured in this tradition ; and it may please us to observe

[1] Who did not forget the importance of the human figure in landscape.

both a Miltonic and a Claudesque quality in their scenes. The selective generalities of Milton's *L'Allegro* are as telling and dignified as those of either of the two French painters; botanical exactitude or detail, vivid colouring or Pre-Raphaelite exactitude, the kind of thing in which Tennyson [1] displayed his virtuosity, is not required, and would introduce into the experience a jarring note. One of the less dignified or valuable moments in Milton's earlier poems is the " purple patch " in *Lycidas*, which has, however, some historical interest as a relique of the " botanic catalogue " which passed from Lorris, via Chaucer and Spenser, to this time. For such reasons, perhaps, it has especially tickled our age, as has the " nectarine and curious peach " stanza from Marvell's *In a Garden*, of which it is by no means the most satisfactory part. Denham, who was but little younger than Milton, had a more mature feeling for the " generalising ideal " which in *Cooper's Hill* he approaches very nigh, more than once. The calm grandeur of his descriptive couplets compares well with Tennysonian antics in *The Daisy* or *The Voyage of Maeldune* :

[1] Cf.
"On candy beaches
A milky-bell'd amaryllis grew." (*The Daisy*.)

Or—

" Millions of roses that sprang without leaf or thorn from a bush
. . . all-coloured plums and . . . golden masses of pear
And the crimson and scarlet of berries that flamed upon bine and
    vine."   (*The Voyage of Maeldune*.)

> " My eye descending from the hill surveys
> Where Thames among the wanton vallies strays,
> Thames, the most lov'd of all the Ocean's sons.
>
> . . . . . .
>
> The stream is so transparent, pure and clear
> That had the self enamour'd youth gaz'd here
> So fatally deceived he had not been.
>
> . . . . . .
>
> But his proud head the airy mountain hides
> Among the clouds ; his shoulders and his sides
> A shady mantle clothes."

The last of these three fragments has already been quoted by Miss Manwaring to illustrate landscape description at an early stage ; but *Cooper's Hill* is chiefly concerned with more human associations, history, myth, and the excitement of staghunting.

The peopling of any scene with classic sprites, whether gods or *putti*, is a sign of the same thing—the humanisation of nature, the adornment of it with beings like, and created by, man; this and the linking up of contemporary richness with the richness of a past polite age, made classical allusion a much less pedantic and mechanical thing than we may suspect; personifications and transplanted Attic deities had a double value: and we have but slender grounds for suspecting that Hamilton (1704–54) wrote—

> " A cherub first, in prime of years,
> The champion fortitude appears,"

feeling less poetically inclined or assenting to a more uninspired automatism than Coleridge when he recounted improbable things of an albatross. Of the execution, the concrete expression of the mood, I say nothing : leaving it aside, we may admit that Coleridge excites us because he does not use language, as Hamilton does, which we have learnt, somewhat blindly, to abhor ; his idiom happens to have stimulated our parents and us, but our grandchildren may very well prefer the other.

In Cowley's works may be traced yet another of the threads of the classic warp—the demand for order. An admirer of Bacon, and of Hobbes, who civilised his "learned America," he rests when he can beneath the right Porphyrian tree. In his address to Davenant he reflects on the reintroduction of good order and humanity into heroic poetry :

"Methinks heroic poesy till now
Like some fantastic fairy-land did show.
Gods, devils, nymphs, witches and giants' race
And, all but man, in man's chief work had place."

(He is thinking of the more fantastic and even Gothic decoration which Davenant, referring to Spenser, deplores for its dream-like feverishness.)

"Thou, like some courtly knight with sacred arms
Dost drive the monsters hence, and end the charms,
Instead of those dost men and manners plant."

The propriety of Bacon's style which "does, like Thames, the best of rivers, glide when the god does not rudely overturn but gently pour the crystal urn" appeals to him. It is the aim of his own couplet : and even his conceit is kept in hand,[1] just as the

[1] "The crystallising of the classical creed goes on regardless of euphuism, earlier and later, of Marinism in Italy . . ." etc., Saintsbury, *History of English Criticism.*

characteristic exuberance is present, but controlled in all Baroque work of merit. The first stanza of *The Muse*, as flamboyant a piece as anything of Cowley's, is certainly far removed from the solid conciseness of Bacon's essays : yet they belong, if not to the same species, to the same genus, as might be said of St. Paul's Cathedral and the Church of Santa Croce at Lecce. His couplet has been called tame, which is to say, amongst other things, that it was not rough. It is like the "learned America" aforesaid, civilised, bevelled to an extent that certainly deprives it of the harsh vigour of Hall or Donne. Taking at a venture some lines from the *Davideis* (IV)—

> " Victorious arms through Ammon's land it bore,
> Ruin behind, and Terrour marched before.
> Where'er from Rabba's towers they cast their sight
> Smoke clouds the day, and flames make clear the night.
> This bright success did Saul's first action bring ;
> The oil, the lot, and crown, less crowned him king,"

and setting beside them this from Donne's *The Storme*—

> " England to whom we owe what we be, and have,
> Sad that her sonnes did seeke a forraine grave
> (For Fates or Fortunes drifts none can soothsay
> Honour and misery have one force and way),"

we may clearly remark the effect of the " taming " process, which did not mean that posterity was to reduce the couplet to mere order and nothing else, to refine it away, in fact, but that it was being prepared as a responsive instrument for the hands of a Dryden and a Pope.

In Waller there was far less conflict between metaphysical and Augustan technique ; " Augustan," because with him, Cowley and Denham, the tide of reasonable verse named after that age sets strongly in ; with his obvious bent for neatness and smooth simplicity, he was able to avoid mannerisms, that tempted Cowley to descend from weight to heaviness, and so used the couplet more cleanly than many of Dryden's seniors. He was, as Aubrey notes, a refiner; his periods are nicely pointed and so ordered that they end with the sharpest couplet of the group.

His verse on St. James's Park illustrates this and other features, notably the attitude of his time toward natural objects. The picture of the park is opulent, crowded, and as daring as anything that might have been painted between Rubens and Thornhill. The composition, enriched with gallants dancing and bathing, a flock of fowl darkening the sky, silver fishes playing by gilded barges, ladies angling in a crystal lake, Cupids on billows, and sea-nymphs entering " with the swelling tide," is in the grand manner, a large canvas with a flourish in its treatment, yet, as all things in the grand manner should be, never vague or untidy. The park, rather than the wilderness, typifies nature methodised, and is saturated as here with human associations. It may be noticed that the trees are estimated chiefly for the convenience of their shade (the first thought that occurred to Cowper when the poplars were felled), but that it is quite possible to write beautifully of the purely utilitarian :

> " In such green palaces, the first kings reigned,
> Slept in their shades, and angels entertained.
>
> . . . . . .
>
> Free from th' impediments of light and noise
> Man, thus retir'd, his nobler thoughts employs.
> Here Charles contrives the ordering of his state."

The dexterity of the technique points forward to Pope, and is part of what Mr. Hulme disapproved ("Romanticism and Classicism" in his *Speculations*), representing the imposition of that discipline which he censures and calls "formalism," upon fiery and delectable shapes. Part of it is prosodic, but the rest consists largely of the very practice of selective generalisation that is one of the articles of Augustan faith. It is unnecessary to describe trees more elaborately than to call them "green palaces"; the remainder is constructed with restraint and vividness out of the record of acts or processes associated with the trees. Only one colour is mentioned, but an effect of much brilliance and colour persists; whereas in the colour scheme of Tennyson's verse (v. *supra*) the effects, through sheer *embarras de richesse*, are soon dispersed.

It was to Davenant, who got them from the Frenchmen, that the introduction of the new ideas concerning heroic poesy was chiefly owing. Elevation was the keynote; "I believe," he writes, "I have usefully taken from courts and camps the patterns of such as will be fit to be imitated by the most necessary men ; and the most necessary men are those who became principall by prerogative of blood. . . . The common crowd, of whom we are hopelesse, we desert, being rather to be corrected by laws. . . . Nor is it needfull that Heroick poesy should be levell'd to the reach of common man." If Davenant was a publican's son, he should have been in a position to judge. At all events this aristocratic conception was certainly of value ; it helped to render possible the spaciousness and loftiness that is repugnant in general to democratic, and especially English democratic art, which, even if it has space, is tempted to waste it on elaborations of detail ; and it is a doctrine allied to that of preferring generalities and selection in art, of that large treatment that requires plenty of room.

Of selection Davenant, defending rime against Sir Robert Howard, and quoting the perennial *ut pictura poesis*, observes that artists take from the natural object " so much only as will make a beautiful resemblance of the whole." Davenant, who, according to Suckling's rhyme, swore even at an Alderman, may have been a snob, but he produced *Gondibert* which, popular prejudice or no, compares very favourably with the hebetudes of *The Life and Death of Jason* ; his prose style, of which there are, alas ! but too few examples, exhibits not merely the power to organise his thoughts in long and balanced sentences, but virility and politeness in a combination that renders ridiculous the rough Gothic *fortissimo* of a Ruskin.

Dryden, following Bellori in his *Parallel of Poetry and Painting*, proceeds to "give away" the oft-repeated theory of the imitation of nature. The two arts are "not only true imitations of Nature, but of the best Nature, of that which is wrought up to a nobler pitch. They present us with images more perfect than the life in any individual; and we have the pleasure to see all the scattered beauties of Nature united in a happy chemistry, without deformities or faults." Thus we are inducted to the elevation of that heroic poesy which was not the least of Dryden's splendours. The connection between the two appears in the *Essay of Heroic Plays*, during the scrutiny of Davenant's *Siege of Rhodes*, when we are told that " the laws of an heroic poem did not dispense with those of the other, but raised them to a greater height, and indulged him a further liberty of fancy, and of drawing all things as far above the ordinary proportion of the stage, as that is beyond the common words and actions of human life" (Ed. W. P. Ker).

How to reconcile the "humanising" of nature with a theory that bids us imitate something almost superhuman and supernatural? How can the proper study of mankind be man, with such rules? The answer seems to be that, from the homocentric point of view, man has the right and the power to improve upon nature; it is the most human of gestures, in the performance of which the artist proved his claim to the title, emphasised by Sidney, of "maker." He may thus both confirm man in the realisation of his potentialities and conduct him, intellectually, toward further triumphs :

" True wit is Nature to advantage dress'd,
What oft was thought, but ne'er so well express'd ;
Something, whose truth convinc'd at sight we find,
That gives us back the image of our mind."

Upon such notes was played the overture of the eighteenth century. John Elsum, a reader of Bellori and Dufresnoy, who returned again and again to the necessity for good deportment in art, would also have nature dressed to advantage, as his *Art of Painting* (1702) informs us. " I laugh at those *that think every Natural Model is good*, as if Nature to show her greatness and perfection, had made no errors concerning its Beauty, for some of her works are not thoro'ly finisht, and therefore good artists do frequently lend her their helping hand as *Zeuxis* did of old."

Nature, then, was to be adorned : but what was she ? Locally, she was often a delicious background for *fêtes champêtres* and Claudesque groups; viewed more widely she was not merely everything material but also, as the ingenious Mr. Wolseley states in his preface to Lord Rochester's *Valentinian* (1685), general notions and abstracted truths, such as exist only in the minds of men, and in the property and relation of things one to another ; and so if man was part of the universe of nature—or Hobbes

—he was the only part capable of dressing her to advantage, of altering or modifying. With such aims in sight, rules are inevitable; law is requisite for good governance, if nature is to be set in order; and it is sometimes the poor pedant's task to frame the code and be damned for it, like Rymer, while the flaming genius, started by the rules on a certain course, is praised if he outstrips it; and it is right that he should be. But let us give Rymer his due for a great deal of sound sense. "A poet is not to leave his reason, and blindly abandon himself to follow fancy, for then his fancy might be monstrous, and please nobody's maggot but his own" (like modern "introvert" art); "but reason is to be his guide, reason is common to all people" (let us hope so) "and can never carry him from what is natural."

The excellent underlying idea cannot be mistaken: Rymer is attempting (*Tragedies of the Last Age*, 1678) to find a suitable, nay, a possible basis for communication, and finds reason. Mr. Richards tells us to-day that "the use of past similarities in experience and the control of these elements through the dependence of their effects upon one another, make up the speaker's, the active communicator's gift" (*Principles of Literary Criticism*, chap. xxii). Here is also a search for communication based on the intelligent use of experience and similarity in experience. The reason which can never carry a man from what is natural is, we may guess, not far removed from the "adjustment to the actual world in which we live" that Mr. Richards prescribes for us; in maladjustment we breed our own maggots. Private experiences require to be judged by the norms of a relevant general experience, and to be universalised in some sense before they are artistically valuable.

Rymer was, it is true, carried away by his "reasonable-natural" idea which came no doubt, as Mr. Richards suggests, from Aristotle's ennobled type; but when he was shocked, as Voltaire was, at Shakespeare's savagery he was not, with all deference to Professor Saintsbury, merely stupid; he was overstating a defensible argument on behalf of law and order; the stability of the type has as much right to consideration as the mobility of the characteristic; and our claims to understand Shakespeare, through our cult of the characteristic, analytical psychology and other apparatus, as the Augustan dullards could not, are far from infallible. There is no doubt that some of us err in overestimating the emotive and unreasonable elements, even if the dullards erred in underestimating them.

Lastly, Rymer derives to some substantial extent from Hobbes, as one may gather from his distinctly mechanistic view, or in particular from his demand for a reason or discretion to control the fancy if not the foolish fantastical. "Judgment," said Hobbes, "begets the strength and structure of a poem"; armed with which notion, Rymer trudged manfully through the valley of the shadow of Elizabethanism.

His historical value, at least, must be recognised. We may claim this also for Sir William Temple, an author of more imposing presence, but neither a minute nor a deep critic. His *Essay on Poetry* (1690) is worth throwing into the scale on the classic side of the beam for his insistence on good sense and judgment, on " the fire, the hammer, the chisel and the file," and on " wit." " Without the forces of wit all poetry is flat and languishing ; without the succours of judgment 'tis wild and extravagant." Hobbes did not, then, live in vain.

The conception of an ideal, a correct type, an absolute, universal, and necessary beauty by which individual instances should be judged, is Boileau's ; and Boileau is also the evangelist of reason:

" Aimez donc la raison ; que toujours vos écrits
　Empruntent d'elle seule leur lustre et leur prix."

Art derives from nature what is universally accepted as true ; and such an artistic representation gives a pleasure which is reasonable, i.e. into which reason enters. So we gather from his *Art Poétique* which Dryden recast, with national allusions, in 1680. Boileau's influence on English letters was extensive and fairly long-lived. After Dryden and Oldham, who followed him in his *Art of Poetry*, Pope exclaimed :

" More happy France ; immortal Boileau there
　Supported genius with a sage's care ;
　　.　　.　　.　　.　　.　　.　　.
　Fancy and sense to form his line conspire
　And faultless judgment guides the purest fire."

Sir Charles Gildon, an opponent of Steele's, upholds French Classicism more strongly, standing firm against the modernism which was introducing a principle of irregularity into art. The regular pieces of French authors are to be held more valuable than the irregular; " are not Boileau, Racine, and the like more entertaining to them " (i.e. the French) " than Alexander Hardy, du Bartas, and the like ? " he inquires. Bysshe comes among the quoters of the *Art Poétique* with " rien n'est plus beau que le vrai, le vrai seul est aimable," etc. On the other side, Sir William Temple, Swift's patron, took up the cudgels against Perrault, who, with Fontenelle, would put Boileau and the moderns above Horace and the ancients.

Sir William did not distinguish himself, and the controversy is mainly valuable because it throws light on the modern or Baroque wing of the neo-classicists, and because it produced Swift's *Battle of the Books*. In this contest the ancients make fearful havoc of the moderns ; but, strange to say, Blackmore cuts a far better figure than Dryden ; Oldham and Afra Behn fall victims to Pindar, and so does Cowley, a relic of whom (*The Mistress*, of course) Venus preserves. In the *Tale of a Tub* (published 1704, written 1696–7), he proceeds further to denigrate Dryden ; his value as a " pro-ancient " must be discounted (*a*) by his personal allegiance to Temple and (*b*) by his personal grudge against Dryden. In the same way his bitter and extremely funny attack on critics in the *Tale of a Tub* is not a sign of an anti-classical attitude towards criticism so much as a hit at Wotton and others.

But the worth of Swift's polemics, taken as a whole, lies, apart from their masterly Rabelaisian style, in the general aim ; he launched them against what was slovenly and superficial in letters, against " the art of being deep-learned and shallow-minded." He protects the discipline of Nature's chief masterpiece—writing well, which cannot be done on the inspiration of a costive diet, want of books, and a just contempt of learning. His and Temple's foe Wotton wrote and published (in 1697) his *Reflections upon Ancient and Modern Learning*, following the lead of Perrault.[1] On the whole, he is inclined to sit on the fence from which he mildly defies Perrault on the one side and Temple on the other. If the former's " politeness " is " a vicious aberration from, and straining of Nature," the latter's impeachment of pedantry is groundless. Every virtuoso is not a Sir Nicholas Gimcrack ; Poussin, Le Brun, and Bernini disprove that artistic decay which Sir William alleges ; on the other hand, the Royal Society has not " outshined or eclipsed the Lyceum of Plato " or the academy of Aristotle. Wotton's arguments are often childish, and he is more timid than Perrault ; but both he and the eminent architect have this much of right on their side—that the modern culture was vigorous and robust, and had the right to assert itself.

[1] His *Parallel between the Ancients and the Moderns.*

CHAPTER IV
THE AGE OF BAROQUE AND THE GRAND MANNER

DECRETALS are now pronounced against " extravagant and senseless objects," against the fantasies that Hobbes deplored. " All ought to aim at sense," which implies, in the aim, economy and balance. There must be no overloading the picture with pompous detail ; " all that is needless carefully avoid." And here, too, we may observe in this antique fortress of classicism a strong redoubt ; " the meanest theme may have a proper style," but—

> " Polish, repolish, every colour lay
> And sometimes add, but oftener take away."

Style is at the root of the matter ; it is not the meanest theme or the meanest flower that blows, which can rouse thoughts that lie too deep for tears, if style is lacking. Trivial incidents are to be eschewed ; " such objects are too mean to stay our sight." These are theories of the grand manner in which style is something other than preoccupation with detail ; it is the reasoned and selective nobility that guides landscapists like Claude, painters of incident in landscape like Poussin, and makers, like Rigaud, of "*portraits d'apparat.*"

To study the pictures of that age is to absorb a great part of its spirit ; we may start with Gravelot's illustrations to Dryden's plays (engraved by Van der Gucht), where neo-classicism triumphs unashamed with tight corsets and low bodices for the women, tunic and buskin for the men, before a setting of obviously Baroque architecture ; the meticulous feeling for period which our romantic training demands, and is allied to Ruskin's " truthful " art, will be gloriously absent. Only a generalising basis for art could make such a thing possible; we might at first disapprove of Van der Gucht's uncompromising burin, but the appeal of this very peculiar beauty cannot be resisted for long ; it conveys so adequately the quality of the dramas it illustrates.

In decorative painting Thornhill is an example, though not the best one could wish, of the employer of generalised and abstract conceptions ; and he is conveniently accessible to English students, at Greenwich. His massive grisaille tritons, his fat and fleshy aerial infants, his copiously personified abstractions, go to prove that the method of interpreting the rules might be, in the days of William and Mary, essentially concrete and remote from the rarer spiritualities. Thornhill deals in flesh and blood, in fish, compasses, ships, and stoutly material emblems ; it is the art of good sense, one purpose of which is that majesty to which Dufresnoy refers :

"And, emulous alone of genuine fame,
    Be grace, be majesty thy constant aim."[1]
This "nobilitas" is more apparent, and freer from the reproach of pompousness in the works of Dryden, Wren, and Purcell. Vanbrugh, like Thornhill, is in danger of overemphasising the quality; his buildings and his comedies alike are too weighted; yet it does not follow that weight itself is undesirable, and could we free our minds of the bias that more immediate events have imparted, we might still find that Vanbrugh could afford us satisfactions that are not to be derived from either Bodley or Bernard Shaw. The jibes of the time about this architectural style such as Evans's—

"Lie heavy on him, earth! for he
    Laid many a heavy load on thee,"

or Swift's—

"At length they in the rubbish spy
    A thing resembling a goose-pie,"

do not damage his reputation: we know his defects which his merits more than counterbalance; but here is evidence that his intelligent contemporaries were aware that he tended to overstress "nobilitas" at the expense of grace. Sir Joshua Reynolds described his merit in architecture, which was, in fact, pictorial. "He perfectly understood in his art, what is the most difficult in ours, the conduct of his background, by which the design and in-

[1] Mason's rendering of "sit nobilitas, charitumque venustas."

vention are set off to the greatest advantage. What the background is in painting, in architecture is the real ground on which the building is erected ; and no architect took greater care that his work should not appear crude and hard—that is, that it did not abruptly start out of the ground without expectation or preparation." The rather pompous gestures of Vanbrugh and Thornhill are not, however, the outcome of conceit but have a valid reason, the attempt to impart the effect of motion ; and this is true not only of much Baroque, but also of some Greek and Roman art.

The Laocoön, an example of crudely expressed kineticism, was revealed to generations, including Thomson, who by æsthetic training were eminently calculated to value it. Lessing uses it as a peg on which to hang (1766) his version of the selective-generalising theory of *pictura* and *poesis*, in which, by the way, he grants the didactic poet (cf. Philips's *Cyder*) special licence to go into detail.

The feeling after stability, which some regard as necessary to the classic attitude, is not necessarily incompatible with features which give the effect of motion ; in the purest Greek there is a contrast which is yet an affinity between the pediment and the rest of the entablature. In Baroque art the kinetic element was everywhere more apparent ; Rubens brought it to an advanced stage, and later painters, like Thornhill, profited by his reconnaissance. There is no reason why it should be labelled romantic, or " Nordic " or " Faustian " ; and indeed, the well-known lines—

" Others lean forth and drink
With eager lips the wind of their own speed,"

were once correctly applied by Professor Gardner, in a lecture, to the Charioteer of Delphi.

This dynamic " kineticism " is traceable in Vanbrugh's rather than in Jones's or Wren's buildings. The two latter sought a quieter *nobilitas*, and the thing that the Elizabethans had failed to achieve, the " greatness of manner " referred to by Addison in his chapter on Architecture in *The Pleasures of the Imagination*. Jones was a true disciple of Vitruvius and Palladio,[1] two authorities who were for architects what Bellori and Dufresnoy were for painters, or Aristotle, Horace, and Boileau for poets. Palladio severely inculcates the pursuit of nature, which means bearing in mind the presumed origins of classic architecture, in the trunks of trees, and so forth ; he deprecated the tendency, evident even in his day (d. 1580), to deviate from simplicity and from " the general and necessary rules of Art and Nature." Fréart, Sieur de Chambray, who wrote *A Parallel of the Ancient Architecture with the Modern*, translated by Evelyn and published in 1664, speaks more violently of " vile and reptile souls " who believe that deviation

[1] His copy of Palladio, with his own notes, was published by Leoni in 1742. In these notes cross-references to Vitruvius are not infrequent.

in detail means invention. Palladio was referring to breaches of taste in minor features ; but Fréart's criticism is more widely applicable. He offers an opening, not for novelty but for invention ; he declares the very images and pure ideas of the ancients (the Greeks, not the Latins) to be the material whence the inventor shall gather inspiration. He would see, not a strange and monstrous alteration of the three orders, but an inventive use of them—he quotes the Pantheon as an example—in their simplest and most abstracted form. Once more, it is an instruction to keep to the type and the universal, though it gives a free hand to Baroque in the use of the orders, if not in their modification. An exponent of the grand manner, he abhorred excess of detail and pettiness, and Addison, who agreed on this point, quoted him in the Sixth Essay on the Imagination ; " to introduce into architecture the grandeur of manner, we ought so to proceed, that the division of the principal members of the order may consist but of few parts, that they be all great and of a bold and ample relievo, and swelling : and that, the eye beholding nothing little and mean, the imagination may be more vigorously touched and affected with the work that stands before it." Such doctrines, of course, damn Gothic effectually.

Inigo Jones, aiming, as he said, at a " solid masculine and unaffected art," established a truly English Palladian tradition. He was influenced but not enslaved by Palladio, and his foreign contemporaries, Mansard and Perrault, had but little effect on him. He was the founder of the English neo-classic school which was still surviving with Nash in the earlier part of the nineteenth century. Wren, in his own and completely English way, carried on the development of the grand, masculine style; he was too bold and original to imitate Palladio with servility, and it was partly owing to this that a Palladian reaction took place among the more timid spirits in the first decade of the eighteenth century. His influence is seen on Hawksmoor, who attempted to compromise between his and Vanbrugh's style, and on Gibbs, architect of the Radcliffe Camera at Oxford.

The eighteenth century produced plenty of Palladian architects, producers of " grand " and certainly dignified work which remained free from rococo frivolities or femininities, unless we impeach the Adam brothers. Dance, who achieved the gloomily sublime in Newgate Jail, is said to have taken a hint from the colossal and gloomy Piranesi (1720–78) in the next phase of a classic evolution. While Wren demanded a symmetrical *nobilitas*, Vanbrugh required balance, indeed, but this might be asymmetrical; and Uvedale Price, as Mr. Hussey points out, mentions grandeur and variety as his two chief aims.

The *quidlibet audendi* which Horace allows to poets and painters is seized upon by Dryden to defend the rhetorical dynamism in his heroic plays. "Are all the flights of Heroic Poetry to be concluded bombast, unnatural, and mere madness, because they" (the readers or critics) "are not affected by their excellence?" he cries indignantly.[1] And in conclusion he argues, "no man will disagree . . . concerning the dignity of style in Heroic Poetry; but all reasonable men will conclude it necessary, that sublime subjects ought to be adorned with the sublimest and consequently with the most figurative expressions."

Quidlibet audendi is a motto of the Baroque, where boldness is expressed through motion and sublimity, the two being inseparable components of this dynamic art. Dryden, while granting the decorum of those stabilising restraints, the unities of action, place and time, with scenes unbroken, claims for himself that manœuvring space which the newer art requires. Neander, in criticising the French, complains that "by their servile observations of the unities of time and place, and integrity of scenes, they have brought upon themselves that dearth of plot, and narrowness of imagination, which may be observed in all their plays. . . . If they content themselves, as Corneille did, with some flat design, which, like an ill riddle, is found out ere it be half proposed, such plots we can make every way regular, as easily as they; but whene'er they endeavour to rise to any quick

[1] *Apology for Heroic Poetry and Poetic License.*

turns and counter turns of plot . . . you see they write as irregularly as we, though they cover it more speciously."

The dangers of " flatness " attended the static rather than the dynamic aspect of neo-classicism ; but England, possibly for the very reasons that Dryden enumerates in the *Essay of Dramatique Poesy* and elsewhere, came off pretty well as regards dearth, flatness, or narrowness ; Dryden's own work in drama, non-dramatic poesy, and prose, was copious and instinct with a lively motion ; the robustness, the bold modern gestures that were yet reminiscent of the ancients, which distinguish him are also distinctive of the Baroque. Flatness and timidity might be found, of course, among minors of the period, as in any other period ; vigour was lost gradually in some departments, e.g., on the stage, when sentimentalities had usurped the fashion after Dryden's death ; but even so, will anyone seriously claim that the first eighty years of the nineteenth century produced better drama than the corresponding part of the eighteenth ? Such " flatness " as may be found in both has little to do with classicism.

In the development of Opera, to which Dryden, with Purcell, contributed much, a very clear inclination towards the dynamic principle is seen. The masque, certainly, had been an entertainment in which music was combined with dramatic poetry ; but music, the least static and most fluid of the arts, had hitherto generally ministered to the words, which it sustained and interpreted.

There is no concession to music at the expense of poetry in *Comus*. But the more declamatory music that, after the Restoration, became the vogue, the music born under French and Italian stars, would neither take second place nor exist on terms of parity; not merely did it take liberties with poetry, but the poet himself began to yield quite frequently to the composer's demands. We find Dryden doing for Purcell what modern writers of popular songs are doing for American dance music. It is not simply that Purcell ignores the rhythm of a lyric and turns the " fly " of " I attempt from love's sickness " into a veritable episode of aviation; Dryden himself in *The British Worthy* writes what is so obviously intended for musical accompaniment that, without the music, set coldly down, some of it reads dangerously like nonsense. In the preface to this play, he goes so far as to apologise for this, after an encomium of Purcell; " the Numbers of Poetry and Vocal Music are sometimes so contrary, that in many places I have been obliged to cramp my verses, and make them rugged to the Reader, that they may be harmonious to the Hearer: of which I have no Reason to repent me, because these sorts of Entertainment are principally designed for the Ear and Eye; and therefore in Reason my Art on this Occasion, ought to be subservient to his."

The choral parts can, undoubtedly, be rugged to the reader :

PHILIDEL, *singing*.   Come follow, follow, follow me.
CHORUS.   Come follow me.
And me.   And me.   And me.   And me.
   VERSE 2. *Vocal.*   And green-sward all your way shall be.
   CHORUS.   Come follow, &c.
   VERSE.   No Goblin or Elf shall dare to offend ye
   CHORUS.   No, no, no, &c.
No Goblin or Elf shall dare to offend ye.

It is scarcely fair to call libretto claptrap and leave it at that. The libretto of opera has been less rather than more satisfactory since Dryden's day, if we except possible ameliorations like *Pelléas and Mélisande* ; and Dryden was initiating, in a composite, kinetic form of art, an experiment which has yet to be successfully concluded. Finally it may be claimed that opera was following the Masque in its attempt to supply a more concrete and tangible sort of art than could be achieved by poetry alone, music alone, or the non-representational pre-restoration stage, which had developed from non-representational conventions accepted in the Middle Ages. The settings of Masques, if we may judge from Jones's designs, were not so much realistic settings as decorations to make music and poetry more concrete and so satisfy the sense or desire for the outwardness, the " outward ceremony " which Blake called Antichrist, that all Baroque art, with its outwardness more important than its inwardness, may claim to satisfy.

This growing demand for an outward and visible sign appears in a more sceptic, scientific, and even materialistic epoch, when attention is paid to a Bacon or a Hobbes. It goes to explain the gulf between Rubens and Van Eyck; the prevalence of outward, declamatory music like that of Blow or Purcell over, let us say, the more elfin counterpoint of Orlando Gibbons; and the difference between *All for Love* and *Antony and Cleopatra*. It is true that stabilising and rarefying theories, laying stress on the abstract and the ideal, as in Dryden's *Parallel*, lay at the back of practice; but the art itself was stoutly three-dimensional. Romantic poesy may etherealise an actual being into "a *phantom* of delight"; but Parnell presents the abstract Nature as an entirely material deity; we can picture his dame, large, plump, clad in exiguous and fluttering vestments, with her "wanton smiles and airy play":

> "Where'er she turn'd, the pulses beat
> With new recruits of genial heat."

By Dryden's time the articles of classic faith were more precisely defined than at the beginning of the century; and to glance with him at Ben Jonson will be to measure the advance. There is much about Jonson in the *Essay of Dramatic Poesy*; he is praised for relating in his *Magnetick Lady* and *Sejanus*, after the manner of the ancients, certain incidents that would be unseemly if presented; he was, on the whole, "a painful observer of τὸ πρέπον," or the decorum of the stage, and " as he has given us the most correct plays, so . . . in his *Discoveries*, we have as many and profitable rules for perfecting the stage, as any wherewith the French can furnish us." But he is most to be censured for a typically English fault, deplored by Sidney, and flagrant in *Sejanus* and *Catiline*, where he " has given us this oleo of a play, this unnatural mixture of comedy and tragedy." This was unnatural to the neo-classics in their hey-day, because however much such mixtures might occur in real life, in art it would be one of those inconsistencies against which Horace issued a warning, and would be at variance with Aristotle's view that not every kind of pleasure, but only that proper to the species, must be expected from tragedy.

The classic mind appeals to authority; and Aristotle, Horace, Longinus, Boileau, Scaliger, or Rapin, rather than everyday experience, would be authorities for nature. And nature, when imitated by art, was to be methodised according to such rules as ensured decorum. Nature was, in short, made for man, and not man for nature: but the rules which man had made for himself must be obeyed— though not with servility—if a standard of art was to be possible at all. Dryden was doing what every critic, to-day at least, cannot or dare not do— setting his standard before him and so comparing what was to be examined. To create and criticise by rule is the procedure of a classicist, and one which indicates that a state of equilibrium, of settled government, has been reached, as by this time had happened. Jonson, who looked towards the consummation, was rightly judged by its law. But he did not altogether conform to the standard, and Dryden, while evidently anxious to do his best for so staunch an adherent to the forge and file, is not entirely happy about him. Was it that a Gothic strain, such as was still appearing in the architecture of his day, survived in him—that there were cusped and transomed windows to his temple of the Muses ?

Langbaine devotes some pages of his *Account of the Dramatick Poets* (1691) to a defence of Jonson and Shakespeare against the censures of Dryden, whom he misliked. The dispute about Jonson's borrowings is unimportant ; but on the Elizabethan tricks of " clinches " and " playing with words "—which were symptomatic of the age that bred euphuism— he has this to say, that Dryden is not wholly free of it himself, though Langbaine has to go to a comic character (Burr in *The Wild Gallant*) to prove his charges. Dryden might clown in a comedy ; but a clown is not brought into the last scene of *All for Love*. Further, Langbaine points out that Plautus has authorised word play. He is able to put his enemy right, or nearly so, over the origin of blank verse ; the passage in the preface to *The Rival Queens* clearly means that *Gorboduc* was rhymed, and that Shakespeare *invented* blank verse. Had Dryden realised that the blank verse of *Gorboduc* was the new Senecan-classic convention that Shakespeare followed, he might have hesitated over the heroic couplet. As for the Jonsonian wit, with its " clenches "—which, like the wit of other Elizabethans, was not that of gentlemen—" there was ever something ill-bred and clownish in it," Langbaine has no adequate defence.

The later conception of wit, the rapier-thrusting or " sharpness of conceit " in *Absalom and Achitophel*, was soon to culminate in Pope. Wit had passed through the stage of the vivid colouring and complexity of the Metaphysicals, as it were from a red to a white heat ; and it had come through the systematic definitions of Hobbes, for whom it was " a tenuity and agility of spirits." Dryden is not free from the coarser clowning in his comedies, and there is plenty of it in *Limberham* ; but he had also the finer sort. " Honest Shakespeare " was accused by Dryden, who loved him nevertheless, of barbarism, and there was reason for the impeachment. Langbaine does not vindicate him as a polite classic, but pleads that he did his best without the help of Corneille, Rapin, or Aristotle, who had yet to illumine, for modern England, the path of dramatic practice : he was forced to admit the advantages of the French rules, but suggested maliciously that Dryden, had he not known them, would have done no better than Shakespeare. Shall we not agree with him ?

CHAPTER V
POLITENESS AND GOOD SENSE

THE element which we call "good sense" and which we regard as a necessary part of the Augustan "make-up," owed its strength very largely to the teachings of John Locke (1632–1704). Locke weighed down the beam against mysticism heavily, as did Vanbrugh against the Gothic; and complaints have been made in our own more hysteric time that he appealed to man's reason rather than to his emotions. The rational practice of abstraction, of conceiving universals, is of high value to him; brutes abstract not, and the power to do so is the test for humanity. He places clear judgment and deep reason over wit, "the assemblage of ideas, and putting those together with quickness and vanity," he observes faith with a grudging eye and enthusiasm with profound distrust. The philosophy of the here and now lies at the base of Augustan art; and if the Middle Ages had, Timotheus-like, raised mortals to the skies, this later period had drawn down the plumpest and most concrete of angels for man's delectation; of what a Brooke might propose, a Locke would dispose.

Addison, who fell under the enchantment of

Locke, as well as under the discipline of le Bossu,[1] provides a useful gloss (in the *Spectator*, 1711) upon the former's definition of wit. True wit, he agrees, consists in the resemblance and congruity of ideas; but false wit consists in cheaper resemblances and congruities, which were, in fact, the Shakespearian pun or Jonsonian clench, and the Elizabethan trick, admired by Puttenham, of casting poems " into the figures of eggs, axes, or altars." Parnell deprecates this, and the pun, in his *Essay on the Different Styles of Poetry*.

The third kind of wit, which consists partly in the resemblance of ideas and partly in the resemblance of words, he finds to be abundant in Cowley but rare in Dryden. It is the more variegated wit of the Metaphysicals, and marks the transition

---

[1] The Abbé René le Bossu (d. 1680), who, to quote from his translator W. J. (1695, 2nd fuller ed. 1719), defined the epic as " a discourse invented with Art to form the Manners, by Instructions disguised under the Allegories of an important Action, delivered in Verse in a probable, diverting, and surprizing Manner." He went so far as to discover a general proposition from Sallust for the moral maxim on which the *Iliad*, as an epic, according to his theory, was founded: *concordia res parvæ crescunt: discordia magnæ dilabuntur*. For him the epic was didactic.

Addison, though affected by le Bossu, does not always see eye to eye with him; not altogether, indeed, on this particular matter. " Though I can by no means think," he writes in *Spectator*, No. 369, (with le Bossu) " that an Epic writer first of all pitches upon a certain moral . . . and afterwards founds a story to it: I am, however, of opinion, that no just Heroic Poem ever was, or can be made, from whence one great moral cannot be deduced."

between the first and second neo-classic phases, or, if you will, the second between first (Elizabethan) and third (Augustan-Baroque). Like Locke, Addison considers wit a doubtful virtue. Boileau has taught him that no thought can be valuable, of which good sense is not the groundwork ; and the poet who, unable to achieve the majestic simplicity of the ancients, freaks his page with the ornament of wit, is nothing more than the kin of those architectural Goths, who " not being able to come up to the simplicity of the old Greeks and Romans have endeavoured to supply its place with all the extravagances of an irregular fancy." Solid sense and elegant expression were the only things that could redeem our poets from being Gothic, as many of them in Mr. Spectator's opinion then were. Finally, a fourth sort of wit was adumbrated ; that of the opposition of ideas as distinct from their assemblage.

Addison's desire was to cut the cackle and come to a plain and serious art ; the unrestful if spiritual confectionery of Gothic must yield to the Palladian goose-pie, which is a very good thing. He would be a bold man to-day who would talk as coolly as Addison of the meanness of a Gothic Cathedral ; but greatness of manner meant for him the Pantheon at Rome—and he was right. The grand manner is incompatible with cusp and crocket, and with the enthusiastic urge expressed in them. Yet one has an uneasy feeling that for Addison the manner must not be too ostentatiously grand ; the admired kind of imagination is polite, as he himself, in theory and practice, is polite. When he mildly censures Milton for his "unnecessary ostentation of learning" it becomes clear that he is not in sympathy with the braveness, the swagger even, of Baroque enterprise, and that a certain timidity keeps him aloof from displays like the Jovian thunder of Dryden or Pope foining and stabbing in a boudoir : and should he say " avia Pieridum peragro loca," he would do so with safeguards and reservations. If anyone reflects the " static " aspect of Classicism Addison does.

Yet having said these things we must note that the sublime,[1] an important ingredient of Baroque and one which is not necessarily romantic in itself, has a certain value for him. Sublimity, like landscape, was admired throughout the most classical period of English art, and is not a sign of " romantic " decadence ; Buckingham, who held that " Nature's chief masterpiece is writing well," is for the sublime, and Gildon commenting on the word [2] (1721) connects the sublime with the elevated, i.e. with the hymn and the epic, with the " will to civilisation " and with " number and harmony, by which its instructions were conveyed with pleasure."

This last is, of course, too vague ; sublimity implied a particular sort of pleasure—such, for

[1] Cf. various references to the Sublime, and to Longinus, in *Spectator*, Nos. 267—369.
[2] *The Laws of Poetry, etc.*, London (1721).

example, as that of the "number and harmony," and gloom and brightness, of *Paradise Lost*. This increased Addison's admiration of Milton, who was its prime exponent, though for himself a smiling scene is preferable to a gloomy or stupendous: after crossing the Alps in 1700 he felt vastly relieved to see a plain. He had an eye for country scenes, both wild and cultivated—an interest which some view as the beginning of the anti-classical movement. This is absurd; for one thing, landscape had the whole sanction of the ancients, whether Ovid, Virgil, Homer, or the Greek novelists; and for another it was present as a decorative theme, though in varying degrees of prominence, from an early phase of the Renaissance. The polite Elizabethans learnt (as Addison directs those of his day) to observe their own countryside from ancient writers—who happened to be Longus, Achilles Tatius, and others. It became localised by Drayton, Browne, and Denham, and generalised through Milton; Dryden is not oblivious of sylvan scenes (cf. *Ode to the Memory of Anne Killigrew*), and Pope, however much one may minimise the pastorals and *Windsor Forest*, saw a good deal in the comforting terms of a Thames-side meadow. What matters is the method of dealing with landscape; the peopling of it with abstract persons, nymphs, gods, and *putti* is one classic method, the selective generalising process another, though cognate; but both still claim the foreground or centre for man ; and as long as man is recognised as taking nature in, rather than nature as absorbing man, the classic mode is indicated. This is a good test for Shakespeare's romanticism ; Lear in his fury becoming one with furious nature is a romantic figure.

It is just the same with fairies ; the creatures of Dryden's " fairy kind of writing " depend, as he says, " only on the force of the imagination " ; the enlightened Augustan yields nothing to them ; but Shakespeare's fairies have it all their own way, and continue to cast their spells upon us. Addison is wide awake, is determined not to allow Shakespeare to hypnotise the weak, superstitious part of his imagination. " Spell " and " incantation," words which have crept into modern poetic, have nothing to do with the polite ; they are merely Gothic. In *Cato*, a model of polite tragedy, there is no disturbing magic, but instead that rarer thing equilibrium, dearer to the mind of a Chinese sage than to superstitious England. Cato himself is equilibrium personified ; like an immovable rock

> " His towering soul
> Midst all the shocks and injuries of fortune,
> Rises superior, and looks down on Cæsar."

The design is strictly classical, the language correct, the characters conceived in a spacious and original manner ; the propriety of the author's art is such that having shed, with Pope, a few Roman drops, we may leave the theatre now that our emotions are as purified and refined as Aristotle would have required. It is, indeed, a perverse age that extols *Hamlet* and ignores *Cato* ; so obviously indeed is the pendulum at an angle to the perpendicular that one might safely predict a renewal of the attempt to understand the beauty of classical tragedy, with its serenity and purer form, of a time when the work not merely of Addison but of solid if less brilliant craftsmen like Hoole or Whitehead, will receive juster treatment.

Already there are signs of fresh allegiance to Pope, whose more flashing gestures are well calculated to arouse attention ; Pope who, with a fury of delight in his mastery of it, vindicates finally the Aristotle—Horace—Boileau technique. His *Essay on Criticism* is both the lecture and the demonstration ; it is nature methodised as much as Gibb's Camera or learned Poussin's landscape ; it is poetry to anyone who is not deafened with a century of uncouth and agonised cries, whether from Shelleys, Brownings, Masefields or Mews. In those days—

> " We conquered France, but felt our captive's charms ;
> Her arts victorious triumphed o'er our arms.
> Britain to soft refinements less a foe,
> Wit grew polite, and numbers learn'd to flow."

It was for the artist a golden rather than a silver age ; a time when credit might be won for conquering both matter and method. Professor Saintsbury, who so dislikes the neo-classics that one might hesitate to trust him far as a critic of them, sneers at Pope, and particularly at his view of nature, which is, according to him, " the usual, the ordinary, the commonplace." We have already seen, and it goes without saying, that the neo-classic nature was nothing of the kind. Since Rapin it has been definitely " nature methodised " and Pope discloses the secret in two fine couplets :

> " Unerring Nature, still divinely bright,
> One clear, unchanged, and universal light ;
> Life, force, and beauty, must to all impart,
> At once the source, and end, and test of Art."

This is the static aspect of nature as opposed to the changing sort dear to modernity ; the department of ideals, abstracts, and universals. It is in imitation of this nature that we may say " the shapeless rock or hanging precipice " giving, as Claude did, the more abiding essence, and ignoring the casualties of auriculas, birds' nests, and what not. Pope is not merely a " great poet," he is unfailingly efficient ; he forgets, unlike Homer, Shakespeare, Shelley, or Browning, to nod. He is the pediment of the façade that had been building laboriously, with mistakes, rebuildings, and alterations, since the day of great, injured Erasmus ; and it may be edifying for us, too, to see by means of comparison what advance had been made. Fortunately his and Chapman's Homer are at hand. The two extracts that follow (both being translations of the beginning of *Od.*, B. I) show usefully what a century of intensive classicism had done for the couplet, for diction, and for polish :

> "The Man, O Muse, inform, that many a way
> Wound with his wisdom to his wishèd stay
> That wandered wondrous far, when he the town
> Of Sacred Troy had sack'd and shivered down
> The cities of a world of nations
> With all their manners, minds, and fashions,
> He saw and knew."
> CHAPMAN.

> "The man for wisdom's various arts renown'd
> Long exercis'd in woes, oh Muse ! resound,
> Who when his arms had wrought the destin'd fall
> Of Sacred Troy, and raz'd her heav'n built wall,
> Wand'ring from clime to clime observant stay'd,
> Their manners noted, and their states survey'd."
> POPE.

To Lord Kames [1] *The Rape of the Lock* was, in point of versification, the most complete performance in the English language ; and there seems to be little reason—Joseph Warton certainly is not one—why this opinion should be altered. Kames might have added that it is the most perfect rococo poem in the English language. Rococo appears in the refinement, or even sometimes the effeminacy, which ideas of interior or intimate decoration impose upon Baroque ; it is a lighter mood of neo-classicism, kinetic rather than dynamic ; the mood in which Fragonard and Tiepolo painted or Prior composed his epigrammatic trifles. But Kames was too near the phenomenon to recognise it for what it

[1] *Elements of Criticism* (1761).

was. Prior's plump Cupids and Venuses, his young Buckhurst playing with a cat, reflect that spirit of light elegance, that curiously enough affected English art and architecture comparatively little; even in the latter part of the classic age the architects at least preferred with Fréart " the heroick gigantic manner" which " does excellently well in those (i.e. public) places, discovering a certain *masculine* and natural beauty which is properly that the French call *la grand manière*" (sic).

Kames admires Addison almost as much as he does Pope, and takes his side, which happens also to be Blackmore's, against Boileau, in the question of the adornment of art with heathen deities : a profitless discussion which reveals the fact of a confusion of critical issues.

Such a confusion is not absent from the thought of Shaftesbury (1671–1713), the not too docile pupil of Locke. Beauty in art and beauty in personal character were both, for him, good taste, and so the latter beauty is continually tripping up the former. In touching on the danger of non-classical models, he writes : " the more remote our pattern is from anything moral or profitable, the more freedom and satisfaction we find in it. We care not how Gothic or barbarous our models are. . . ."[1] This is calling Gothic immoral ; and he goes on to say that reading about Japan or Turkey instead of about Greece or Rome is as harmful

[1] *Advice to an Author.*

to the taste as the mediæval romances ; in fact the reading of Greek and Roman history may well have given him religious satisfaction.

His method of approach is naïve ; but if any known attempt to square religion and morals with classicism can be praised, Shaftesbury deserves his meed. Moreover, his insistence on the development of vigorous critical spirit as a means of acquiring taste, and his scorn for " those indolent supine authors who . . . reject the criticising and examining art by which alone they are able to discover true beauty. . . ."[1] suggest, as Pope does, that there was in the age of " good sense " not a humdrum adherence to rules and acceptance of the ordinary and commonplace, but a fiery, enterprising spirit, in search of or requiring a definite, authoritative, and established standard of beauty, yet permitting freedom in the search.

He finds the pictorial art severe, its rules rigid ; and here good taste marks out for its own " a Hand happily form'd on Nature, and the Antients." Good taste may force nature in the name of art ; and indeed Nature is scarcely natural until she thus has been methodised. Discernment and selection in the search for the ideal or quintessence, " the real Beauty and VENUS of the kind "[2] is required of the artist ; and besides this, unity and simplicity, and subordination of particulars.[3]

[1] *Miscellany III*, ch. ii.   [2] *Advice to an Author.*
[3] *The Judgment of Hercules.*

In architecture he was a purist and resented, perhaps even more than Palladio or the Sieur de Chambray, the liberties taken by modern baroque designers.[1] He is obviously incensed with Wren, dislikes St. Paul's, and sees in the rapid ascent of spires in the city " much of what artists call the Gothick kind." Both he and Addison stood firm, as Hogarth did later, against the temptation that mediæval art was beginning, though without conviction, to offer. Pope so far succumbed as to write a skit in the Chaucerian manner, and it was not long before the Spenserean bogus antique became quite the mode.

Finally, he might say with Parnell [2]—

" I hate the vulgar and untuneful mind,
  Hearts uninspired, and senses unrefin'd ; "

but, not content to leave the vulgar so, he wished art to be propagated by national and popular education.

His mind was sufficiently agile to leap over the uneven ground of his system of taste ; but poor Blackmore, dull and pious, floundered about so heavily that he attracted the ridicule of his sprightlier contemporaries. Gildon is very sarcastic at his " great parade of words against Aristotle," and at his suggestion that Aristotle may now be discarded as an authority on poetic : Sir Richard's style, he

[1] *A Letter Concerning Design.*
[2] *Essay on the Different Styles of Poetry.*

adds, is a poor advertisement for his modernistic theory (*The Laws of Poetry*, etc.).

Blackmore's warm religious orthodoxy led him so far astray as to embroil him pointlessly with Pope who, he hinted, was " a godless author " ; and for the wits of his time, and especially Swift, he was nothing but venom, because of their " sarcastick and spiteful strokes at religion." The fact was that minds trained on the classical fundamentals of reason and good sense to suspect enthusiastic and kindred symptoms were reasonably sceptical. Shaftesbury (*Miscellany II*) defends scepticism on the grounds that anyone who is a critic is bound not to accept his faith blindly, or dogmatise about it rashly ; and every man of taste is, of course, a sceptic. It is clear, too, from his remarks on enthusiasm a few pages earlier, that he is reluctant to give it much credit. He prefers pagan philosophy to modern hysterics, while Blackmore would have it somewhat the other way. Democritus, Epicurus, and Lucretius are for him " assertors of impiety," and the classic decoration of art, that has now been established for centuries, is to be banished for being heathen. He will never " borrow any embellishments from the exploded and obsolete theology of the ancient idolaters of Greece, Rome, ... or adorn the style with allusions to their fabulous actions. I have more than once publicly declared my opinion, that a Christian poet cannot but appear monstrous in a Pagan dress. . . ."

No wonder the wits grinned; no wonder that "Sharp-judging Adriel," the admirer of Hobbes, had a jibe for him, or that Gay wrote describing how "England's arch-poet"—

> "Undid creation at a jirk,
> And of redemption made damn'd work,
> Then took his muse at once and dip'd her
> Full in the middle of the scripture."

Hobbes was to him an "insulting Briton"

> "Who with contempt on blest religion trod,
> Mock'd all his precepts, and renounc'd his God."

His cosmos is impregnated with the deity; and he seemed, in his *Creation*, to be striving after an idea which would have anticipated the more concrete and scientific findings of Erasmus Darwin, Samuel Butler, and Bergson—that of creative evolution; had the question of "luck or cunning?" been put to him he would have plumped for divine cunning. But he died twenty years before Buffon published, and his ideas are crudely put. Buckingham, a disciple of Hobbes, speaks of his "huge mountain-load of heroical lumber," and conceives nature, in *The Rapture* at least, upon a different plan. Natural laws are decreed by heaven, and therefore to follow nature is to be virtuous; drinking wine and dallying with "some rural nymph, soon taken, soon embraced," are natural and so virtuous actions. This is frivolous but not sentimental paganism; nor is it an incitement to the "return to nature," but merely an amusing apology for a pagan *ens entium*. Disciples of Hobbes might well hold such a view.

Paganism, as well as Deism, is more akin to the mechanic universe than to that of the "pre-creative-evolutionists" one of whom, the mystical Henry Brooke, reminds us in his *Hymn to Universal Beauty* (about 1736) that the author of the universe is not " Nonentity," which may have been the true " *ens* " of a Hobbesian despite any protests, but—

> " . . . He who inaccessible remains,
> Yet omnipresent through all Nature reigns."

He adds a footnote clearly directed against Hobbesianism : " one of the atheistical unaccountable evasions, is to account for the order of Nature by matter and motion." The more materialistic view has been traced in " romantic " or post-Darwinian theory, and considered typical of romantic thought : but it persisted, together with the more mystical theory of immanence (also revived in " romantic " times), during the seventeenth and eighteenth centuries, and cannot be claimed as the exclusive property of either camp, —except that materialistic and sceptic tendencies were certainly fostered, if not originated, in the various phases of the Renaissance. Brooke was, of course, an enthusiast, a pursuer of what the classic who cultivated reason must regard askance ; and the solutions of cosmic problems by a mind under the sway of Behmen could not be regarded as the orthodox or typical solutions of a period of thought in which Hobbes, Shaftesbury, and Locke [1] were revered. And so, if anything, the more pagan, materialistic, and " reasonable " view may be considered the more typically classic.

Despite Blackmore's objections, the tide of pagan poetic flowed strongly in Augustan channels : Sheffield, in *An Essay on Poetry*, conducted a tour up Parnassus hill, at the top of which Virgil and Homer were sitting ; Roscommon (whom Wordsworth scorned) translated the *Epistle to the Pisos*, and had written in his Essay, of Sheffield himself :

" Happy that author whose correct essay
Repairs so well our old Horatian way."

A couplet that sums up the position admirably. Further, he maintained the national spirit which has already been observed, and made out of all foreign imports something characteristic of English classicism.

" The weighty bullion of one sterling line
Drawn to French wire, would through whole pages shine."

Neither Boileau nor Palladio had it all their own way, in practice. The polite Lord Lansdowne (1667–1735), a third preacher of poetic in verse, issued a warning against unnatural flights in poetry ; if the rules were adhered to, poetry had still ample

[1] The grouping of these three names is not meant to suggest that Shaftesbury either held a mechanistic view or that he followed Locke in the direction of a sensational epistemology.

space to soar, without passing into forbidden regions. Even the hyperbole was under the control of laws. At the same time he committed himself on the point of didacticism in verse. Dryden had put pleasure before teaching, but now—

> "Ladies and beaux to please is all the task,
> But the sharp critick will instruction ask."

The critical spirit, which Shaftesbury demanded, was growing in importance ; poetry in the didactic vein was now a vehicle for something more than a moral concealed, or partly so, in allegory ; now that the puritan protests at poetry as the art of lies, and the references to Plato's strictures, which Sidney had been at some pains to explain away, no longer offered any serious menace—some time had passed since Milton[1] had compared Spenser, as a teacher, with Duns Scotus and Aquinas—there was more liberty for the development of the technical poem, of which Davies had already given an example in his *Orchestra* (1596). Although le Bossu, who was much admired in England, had stated his ethical case, Horace, Boileau, and Lucretius, Hobbes's fore-runner, had, amongst others, shown how things useful and speculative might be imparted in good verse, which is poetry for such (may their numbers increase !) as hold that the lyric, the poignant, merely constitute the differentiæ of a species.

There was soon a multiplication of poems

[1] In *Areopagitica*.

describing how a thing is done, whether it be verse-writing, painting, sugar-refining, administering purges, making puddings, or what not ; others, like Darwin's *Botanic Garden*, attempted to demonstrate how or why something happens. Milton and Spenser had written in a different sort of didactic mood ; they did not lose sight of the moral, of the consideration of what we ought to do or think. This, shall we not agree, remains true of Milton, after all has been said or done to redeem him from the stigma of a puritanical pulpiteer. The technical poems of the Augustan phase, and later (e.g. *The Temple of Nature*) contained much that is both curious and beautiful. In Philips's Miltonic *Cider* (1706), there is that detail that a didactic poem requires, but it is neither too finicky, nor disproportionate to the length of the poem ; he adumbrates, with a view to the total effect :

> " Berries and sky-dy'd plumbs, and what in coat
> Rough, or soft-rin'd, or bearded husk, or shell,
> Fat olives, and Pistacio's fragrant nut
> And the Pine's tasteful apple. . . ."

Somerville, a student of Horace and Boileau, and yet a Miltonist in his use of diction and blank verse, which he could follow or caricature at will, offers us in his *Chase* (1735) delights of a rustic opulence refined by the elegance of erudition ; eels, perch, and pike are familiar with Naiads or Tritons ; and the polite stag-hunter, threading Windsor glades, recollects how Denham here charmed once the listening Dryads. The bold flights, the exuberance, of these didactic poets, give the lie to any assertion that timidity, deadness, narrowness, and commonplace were characteristic of the eighteenth century. Few poets to-day would dare to write on the art of preserving health, or the composition of a sack posset ; the view of several of our critics is too narrow to admit of the inclusion of such wealth ; and our *fiscus* is impoverished. We are more likely, perhaps, to side with a theory of Mr. Drinkwater's, lately referred to by Professor Grierson, and say that there is only one kind of poetry, which is lyric ; that poetry's true affinity is music, and " ut pictura poesis " a falsehood.

The then poets might have said, with James Harris (1709–80), that art " is an habitual power in man of becoming the cause of some effect, according to a system of various and well-approved precepts," but, observing those precepts, that there was still ample space to soar, much more indeed than the promoters of the lyric restriction allow us. Erasmus Darwin's *Botanic Garden* and *Temple of Nature*, which appeared in the latter part of the era, are astounding and audacious productions ; and had their author been as skilled a technician in words as he was in science, he might have taken precedence of most didactic writers. As it is, they are magnificent failures, and superior *qua poetry* to many of Shelley's ineptitudes.

Harris's comparison of poetry with music is fruitful ; for him poetry has the advantage because of its utility; it is able to convey practicable themes. Music has its own way of being efficient, and poetry quite another way. When they approach it is not along the path imagined by quasi-mystical theorists, but on the broad trysting ground, the Hyde Park, may we say, of opera and oratorio.

These two forms, Harris has to admit, are not really quite like anything in nature, but their improbability is negligible; they are natural events heightened and intensified by art, as the classic code permits—such an improvement on the original that you must put up, for its sake, with the fact that persons in real life do not go about singing their conversation in arpeggios. He concludes his *Dialogue concerning Art* (dedicated to the Earl of Shaftesbury) by returning to the position that poetry transcends music, and painting also, by reason of its utility. This is coarser than what is implied in the so-called utility theory of beauty enunciated by Hume (1711–76); but under both the principle of nature methodised can, I think, be found to lurk. Hume's hill covered with vines or olive trees and Harris's useful verse are valuable for the use and control of man, who still occupies the centre of the picture. Man's power is proved and aided by them, and not—

> "That universal power,
> And fitness in the latent qualities
> And essences of things, by which the mind
> Is moved with feelings of delight,"

through which Wordsworth " came strengthened with a super-added soul." It should be noted that Harris was an amateur of music and expressed the greatest admiration for Handel.

By this time, that is, before the century was far advanced, certain changes in taste and art were taking place, to mark the development of Baroque. The cult of Milton was increasing—Addison himself contributed to it, and, in connection with it, the classic landscape, derived also from Claude's hesperian hues and learned Poussin, occupied more of the poets' and painters' time—"ut pictura poesis," as Horace and Dufresnoy both observed. But the human figure, in painting, was not relegated to an inferior position ; Harris (once more) admires Salvator for " a most affecting representation of various human figures " in his " Crucifixion of Polycrates," and compares it with Milton's *Il Penseroso* ; while Guido Reni's " Aurora," with its company of youth and beauty, is a " pleasing and animated Allegro." The late classics were coming in for more admiration and to some extent diverted attention from the ancients, who, since the battle of the books, had yielded some ground.

Salvator was a baroque painter, and so, many years later, was B. R. Haydon ; if we would see romantic painting we must first discredit those who would put back the " romantic beginnings " nearly as far as Polygnotus himself, and start fairly with Turner. Landscape and natural beauty are, Harris reminds us, approved of by Virgil and Horace; and this authorised classic taste passed to the modern poets, painters, and landscape gardeners.

There is other evidence that the roots of romanticism were less far-reaching and pervasive than many suppose; the history of architecture abounds in it, and so does that of literature. As late as 1780 Harris declared that English style "reached not a *classical purity* sooner than Tillotson, Dryden, Addison, Shaftesbury, Prior, Pope, Atterbury, etc."; which indicates what ideals were held long after Thomson had produced the Miltonic *Seasons* and the Spenserean *Castle of Indolence*. Nevertheless, there was some pre-romantic unrest before the *Lyrical Ballads*, whether it was fostered by the appearance of Ossian, by Joseph Warton's attack on Pope, or by the quaint strangeness of that Gothic which the soberer spirits deplored. But the playful or serious pastiches of Spenser were sometimes nothing more than diversions of the neo-classics, as with Cambridge, Bedingfield (*The Education of Achilles*)[1] or Bishop Lowth (*The Choice of Hercules*)[1]; and sometimes they were metrical essays in which the Augustan-Georgian mind scarcely disguised itself. The "Hebrid Isle" stanza of *The Castle of Indolence* has been pounced upon eagerly by romantics seeking after a sign, and having that, they would appropriate the whole of *The Seasons*. It is the pictorial element, perhaps,

[1] Bell's *Classical Arrangement of Fugitive Poetry*, 1790.

that gives rise to the illusion that this poem is in the romantic mood ; but Thomson's method here cannot be questioned. The description in *Winter*, to take one of numerous examples—

> " The horizontal sun
> Broad o'er the south, hangs at his utmost noon
> And ineffectual strikes the gelid cliff,"

tells us in words what Claude would have told on canvas ; he would have seen, not as Ruskin, the tertiary cliff with inclined strata, or glacial curvatures, particular after particular, but in all its essential and generalised dignity, the gelid cliff.

Liberty places Thomson, beyond all doubt, with the classics :

> " From the depths
> Of Gothic darkness, springs another day."

" Cooler thought, well-reason'd," then operates until " Athenian laurels still afresh shall bloom." Sculpture cleans her chisel from Gothic rust, and, inspired by " the best proportions . . . that ever Greece beheld "—in short, by the Laocoön, recommences her activities through Michelangelo. In Part V of this work are reviewed, with admiration, the Frenchman, Boileau, restoring ancient taste, Corneille's Roman soul, elegant Racine, Molière's well-judged wit, and Poussin, who restores " ancient design that lifts a fairer front." He is quite correct in estimating Poussin as a classicist. The admiration for sublimity and darkness, which did much for the reputations of Milton and Salvator, also became very prominent at this stage. Pomfret, a contemporary of Dryden's, presented, in some pindarics on the General Conflagration, with all the proper restraint and universality of diction, a fine lyric portrait of the world burning to death:

> "The trembling Alps abscond their aged heads
>   In mighty pillars of infernal smoke,
>   Which from the bellowing caverns broke,
> And suffocates whole nations as it spreads."

And in Yalden's *Hymn to Darkness* large beauties and a sublimity of this general kind are also seen. Burke devotes a substantial portion of *On the Sublime and Beautiful* to darkness, and maintains that " the great ought to be dark or gloomy " (1756). Lastly, Kirke White thus addresses " H. Fuseli, Esq., on seeing engravings from his designs ":

> " Mighty magician! Who, on Torneo's brow,
> When sullen tempests wrap the throne of night
> Art wont to sit and catch the gleam of light
> That shoots across the gloom opaque below."

Fuseli was a late exponent of this baroque device (cf. his plate *The Creation of Eve*, about 1803), and expressed humorous disapproval of " Mr. Constable." Ossian, with his " solemn and awful grandeur," would be likely to appeal to admirers of the sublime, including Blair, who, setting out to compare him with Homer, finds him superior in dignity of sentiment, and more refined than Virgil.[1]

Going on to apply the Aristotelian tests, Blair finds that Ossian preserves the rule of the Unity of Epic Action, and that it is, in fact, a model of strictly classical construction. The ingenious Macpherson had seen to that. There is something pathetic in the spectacle of a poem—an insidious and corrupting thing steeped in that glamour which was too soon to intoxicate the decorous Muses—receiving admission to the Georgian Helicon on purely classical qualifications. Beside this portent the question of forgery or authenticity fades into insignificance.

Blair knew not what he did ; he admired Ossian because he was a Scotsman, and not because he was a seceder. His sympathies were entirely Augustan, and he delights in Dryden's prose. " The restoration of King Charles II," he says,[2] " seems to be the era of the formation of our present style." His views on taste are impeccable ; that of Longinus (who influenced Boileau) is most delicate, that of Aristotle most correct ; while in modern times we have Mr. Addison and Dean Swift. Yet it is symptomatic that he, like Addison, admires Milton, whose poetic imitators were now increasing, and points out that to have preferred Cowley and Waller, Suckling and Etherege, was a fault in taste. Mil-

[1] *A Critical Dissertation on the Poems of Ossian*, 1762.
[2] *Lectures on Rhetoric and Belles Lettres*, xviii.

ton's work was pure renaissance, its nobility such as no amateur of the sublime could neglect ; but Shakespeare was very far from this, and it is not surprising to find Blair, late in the century if not as late as 1767, repeating the classic view of him : that he grotesquely mixes Tragedy with Comedy, that he has the numerous blemishes of strained thoughts, affected witticisms, etc.

The sublime, so much affected in Georgian times, he tracks with detective enthusiasm. Primarily, it is vastness, spaciousness ; the very infinite which (Mr. Hulme assured us) betrays one to romanticism. But again, it depends upon how the infinite is handled, and Professor Blair handles it with classic sobriety ; the test is, that he is not going to let himself be carried away by the infinite but merely by Mr. Macpherson. Then there is darkness (he cites Dryden for this), the solemn and the awful ; and in the realm of ethics there is the sentimental sublime (which includes the spirit of heroic drama) ; magnanimity and high moral virtue, or greatness of character without any virtue, belong here. In regard to the flavouring of terror in the sublime, he disagrees with Burke ; grandeur need not alarm. According to Longinus's rules, it need not ; but Longinus does not distinguish clearly enough, for Blair, between the sublime and the elegant. The merely beautiful (!), gay, and elegant, cannot be sublime. Akenside's *Pleasures of the Imagination* (a sound piece of Baroque) is the kind of thing he desiderates and quotes ; in opposition to this Sublime is the Frigid, in which Sir Richard Blackmore abounds ; while another opposite, the Bombastic, occurs, he regrets to say, in Shakespeare—which is perfectly true.

Beauty, slightly inferior to sublimity, is more "grateful and comforting," and does not elevate one's mind too much ; for Blair regularity is one, but not the only nor the chief one, of the ingredients of this sedative. For him, Hogarth with his Spiral has not lived in vain ; "a straight canal is an insipid figure in comparison of the meanders of rivers." Variety and motion are great aids to Beauty at this stage of things.

Orthodox views on the sublime improving on Longinus were well maintained in the middle of the century ; Alexander Gerard, another *decus et lumen* of Aberdeen, won a prize in 1756 for his *Essay on Taste*, in the early pages of which he laments that "when genuine elegance . . . has long been the fashion, men sometimes grow weary of it, and imitate the Chinese or revive the Gothic taste. . . . The pleasure of novelty is, in this case, preferred to that which results from real beauty." The sublime, he continues, requires largeness, and simplicity, and proportion. "Works in the Gothic taste, crowded with minute ornaments, fall as much short of perfect beauty, by their disproportion, as by their deviation from simplicity."

Refinement of taste is required for the appreciation of Greek architecture or Italian music. "The polite and knowing are chiefly touched with those delicacies which would escape the notice of a vulgar eye." The "wildernesses" of nature are admitted into this correct æsthetic scheme, when imitated by art—after variety has been "passed" by Dufresnoy and Hogarth. Gerard admirably expounds the late classical attitude; while, on the one hand, he demands authority, on the other he will have no confinement by rule or servile acquiescence; there must yet be room to soar, if one may reiterate the phrase.

Burke *On the Sublime and Beautiful* (1756) is disappointingly shallow, though the book has its value as an attempt to set up criteria for taste, to transfer æsthetic from the ethical to the rational and even psychological field, and to define taste itself, which is "partly made up of a perception of the primary pleasures of sense, of the secondary pleasures of the imagination, and of the conclusions of the reasoning faculty." Wrong taste, a defect of judgment, springs largely from stupidity and ignorance, and sensibility alone will not make a good judge. His interest in the darkness, magnificence, and terror of the sublime enhances his admiration for Milton's Satan, "in shape and gesture proudly eminent," Virgil's Fame, and Homer's Discord. His fears that the sublime may pass over to the grotesque when painting interprets poetry seem to be justified by little more than the pre-classical or transitional art that interpreted the

Scriptures, when Hell was certainly rendered with grim humour. Rubens could hardly be said to have failed " to give us clear representations of these very fanciful and terrible ideas."

English "Renaissance" painting developed very slowly: under the Tudors and Stuarts the import of continental masters continued, but an English school of painting, from miniature painting and engraving, which flourished here as distinct in the seventeenth century, or a really great English master, were still to seek. Hogarth at length fulfilled the functions of theorist and practician. His *Analysis of Beauty* (1753) rests chiefly on the principle of the serpentine curve in art, and he is at some pains to demonstrate that neo-classic art accords with it; that Michelangelo referred to it in a cryptic utterance repeated by Lamozzo, and that Dufresnoy admires the serpent-like and flaming form. The spiral principle is not, then, a sign of decadence, but has been known and acted on throughout the age of renascent art. It is related to painting rather than to architecture; and when the spiral walk or curved plantation began to appear in landscape gardening it merely meant that garden design was passing from an architectural to a pictorial basis—at least, this contention is borne out by the now recognised fact that the landscape gardeners derived inspiration from Claudesque painting; and there is nothing inherently decadent or romantic about that.

Hogarth orients himself well in setting out the points ; he defends the pine-apple in architecture, that crown of so many late classic gate-posts ; censures the Laocoön group for sacrificing verisimilitude to pyramidal design—had it been serpentine, the tale would have been different ; and refers to the " pleasing kind of horror " in huge, shapeless rocks (one aspect of sublimity) and the softer reverence (another aspect) felt for large groves and palaces. We may note the milder kind of sublimity in the " evening " or " churchyard " moods of Gray and Collins, in the landscapes of the Smiths of Chichester or Richard Wilson ; while the severer frowns at one from Salvator or Piranesi, from the plates of William Blake, from Yalden's *Hymn to Darkness*, or Milton's *Pandemonium*.

Hogarth was recognised by Lloyd, at least, as " first of every clime for humour keen or strong sublime." And from the evidence of his comparison of St. Paul's with Westminster Abbey, alone, we might judge him to be no friend to the Gothic ; but elsewhere he urges that the elegant spiral is not associated with the gods of " barbarous and Gothic nations," as it is with the classical gods ; while the " pagods " of China, also devoid of the spiral, are notable merely for their meanness.[1]

[1] Lloyd tilts at both in *The Cit's Country Box*, 1757:
" The trav'ler with amazement sees
A temple, Gothic or Chinese,
With many a bell and tawdry rag on,
And crested with a sprawling dragon."

The spiral and the sublime in its varieties fell within the classic terrain from which, however, persons of taste might be led astray into Gothicism, like Joseph Warton, or Chinoiserie [1] ; like Sir William Chambers, who was, when away from Kew, a very competent neo-Palladian. Hogarth wrote perhaps a trifle severely of the Chinese taste, which was well enough in a drawing-room ; his contempt almost takes the form of his refusing to try to understand it at all.

On other heads his fairness and good sense are just such as one would expect from so balanced a genius ; thus, he is not going to admire " our ancients " merely because they are ancient. This is a valuable orientation ; love of the ancient for its own sake, for the glamour of time, cannot be a neo-classic attitude, but belongs to the cult of old, unhappy, far-off things. In his distinction between the comic and the beautiful, elegance and greatness (or grandeur) are the tests. A man in a sack jumping across a stage, being inelegant, makes the audience laugh ; but a vase of elegant design, were it to indulge in the same antics, would merely cause surprise. Certain grotesques sanctioned by Græco-Roman usage, sphinxes, sirens, centaurs, and the more modern griffin, are beautiful ; but about those bodiless child cherubim that were the spawn of Renaissance art, and, according to legend, a posthumous problem for Dr. Keate, Hogarth feels

[1] Cf. his *Philosophy of Rhetoric*, pub. 1776.

doubtful ; there is an absurdity in " an infant's head of about two years old, with a pair of duck's wings placed under its chin, supposed always to be flying about and singing psalms."

He might be summed up as a progressive classicist who has enlarged the bounds set about beauty by rule, and will not defer unduly to the ancients ; from such a spirit came what was best in the art of the Georgians. Richard Payne Knight (1753–1824) opposed the Hogarthian line of beauty, in the first years of the next century, partly from a mere emotional reaction, and partly from the fact that he, like others of his time, was affected by the Græco-classical revival, that Counter-reformation of taste to which they also contributed. Zigzag walks and serpentine canals, Hogarthian things, were repugnant to common sense ; the Greek sculptors produced their masterpieces without artificial rules and " lines of beauty." Knight admired classic art, deprecated the vulgarising effect of the French Revolution on taste, i.e. in promoting the vulgar-romantic, but demands more freedom from " system." If Homer were to listen to the professors who practise scholastic dissection upon him he would call them prating old fools. He is annoyed with Aristotle, but in sympathy with Longinus.

His view of the Augustan Age is curious ; he maintains that the imitative arts (painting and sculpture) were at their lowest when hoop and periwig held the fashion ; but that taste in literary composition, being independent of dress, then "attained a degree of purity and perfection only surpassed by that of the finest ages in Greece and Rome." Yet he has nothing against Gothic and indeed defends it and sees dignity in it, so long as it is properly used. But modern enterprise, whether in the Grecian or Gothic style, might be offensive : the house of an English gentleman was neither a Grecian temple, nor a Gothic abbey, nor a feudal castle. He found faults as well as dignity in Vanbrugh, and his heart, despite a tolerance for pointed styles, was with pure classic or pre-Palladian architecture. Finally, he divided into three what is now generally dichotomised, thus :

(*a*) Classic : scenery (*à la* Claude) with ruined buildings, fragments of sculpture and broken columns, which set up trains of ideas, imagining celebrity and culture ; the whole scenery around receives an accessory character.

(*b*) Romantic : wild, abrupt, fantastic ; endless intricacies discover at every turn something new and unexpected.

(*c*) Pastoral : neat and comfortable, with a plain and simple but not rude and vulgar peasantry ; cultivated fields.

All of which scarcely increases our confidence in him as an æsthetician ; it being possible to treat any of the three classically or not.

CHAPTER VI
GEORGIAN DEVELOPMENTS

IN 1756 Joseph Warton wrote Dr. Young a letter in which he said, " I revere the memory of Pope, . . . but I do not think him at the head of his profession."[1] After which the skittles fell copiously ; Donne and Swift, Fontenelle and Boileau, down they came. Was Warton bowling at them with a romantic theory of poetry ? Not in the least ; he was armed with a missile from Horace himself :

" Non satis est puris versum perscribere verbis."

" It is amazing [that] this matter should ever have been mistaken when Horace has taken particular . . . pains to settle . . . the opinion." In short, it is Horace who demands imaginative and essentially poetic faculties, such as are possessed by Milton, Homer, and Virgil—and by Spenser and Shakespeare. Thus subtly does the Accuser quote the canons of criticism for his purpose. He proceeds to demand for the highest type of poetry the sublime and the pathetic [2]—this last the pet of

[1] *Essay on the Genius and Writings of Pope*, 1756-82.
[2] Addison—to compare this with the older view—had divorced pathos from sublimity. He argued from Longinus that the pathetic

Steele, La Chaussée, and the sentimentalists—and applies to Pope Voltaire's criticism of Boileau : both are poets of reason, but not of sublimity or pathos. But we have seen that the last two elements are the test for poetry ; and on this basis he makes the following classification :

Class A, 1 (pathetic and sublime) : Spenser, Shakespeare, Milton.

Class A, 2 (slightly pathetic and sublime) : Dryden, Donne, Denham, Cowley, Congreve.

Class B (wit, elegant taste, etc.) : Prior, Waller, Parnell, Swift, Fenton.

Class C (mere, though sometimes mellifluous, versifiers) : Pitt, Sandys, Fairfax, Brome, Buckingham, Lansdowne.

The classification is significant and not wholly acceptable to-day, though it were so yesterday. Warton was right in reminding his contemporaries that Horace looked for something more than " pura verba," the something that Cliché (useful nymph) calls " the divine fire," but psychological criticism more accurately, perhaps, defines. Warton went wrong in calling it the Sublime and the Pathetic. Led astray by new doctrines of the Sublime and the Sentimental, the inwardness of which he missed, he helped to lead others astray.

was not essential to the sublime, and that " those who excel most in stirring up the passions very often want the talent of writing in the great and sublime manner " (*Spectator*, No. 339).

This myopia blinded him somewhat to the fires in Pope, and incidentally to the function of pathos in Pope, which, he seems to believe, wit must repel, as oil water. The pathos of Pope's Pastorals, for instance, is witty. After much discussion he places him at the top of Class A2, with a warning that Young and Thomson have equalled him, but that he has written nothing as sublime as Gray's *Bard*. He eagerly welcomes the slightly " gothic " suggestion in *Eloisa to Abelard* which is pronounced the most truly poetical thing that Mr. Pope has done, " so picturesque are the epithets."

Picturesque is now in the ascendant ; but we must not forget that it has the blessing of Horace and Virgil. Warton did not advise the abandonment of classicism, but merely maintains that Bossu, Boileau, and their like are not " sufficient to form a taste upon, without having recourse to . . . the Grecian writers." At the same time he has feeling for what, in Salvator Rosa, he calls " romantic," which he finds also in Thomson's *Seasons*. To be romantic one must, surely, look out, in the appropriate mood, through magic casements, yielding to a spell. Thomson has no such vision, and Salvator is certainly composing rather theatrically his " sublime " pieces in the baroque taste. The sublime, as treated by both, is, as attempts have been made to show, not romantic ; but it is, no doubt, this very sublime so treated that Warton means ; the thing which, he agrees, Harris could, but

Longinus could not, define. It is lively and *picturesque* in Homer, according to the Georgian estimation for which the picturesque was daily increasing in importance.

The Gothic taste and the Gothic age were for him not necessarily inseparable; he champions the Renaissance against the barbarous Middle Ages, when bishops could not write and the Feast of the Ass was celebrated: he may affect the shrines and grots of Pope's *Eloisa*, but he holds no brief for the times, as such, that true romantics (Ruskin, Chesterton) so lovingly and debatably recreate. The spirit he would revive is that of the Renaissance of Erasmus, who drove those holy Vandals off the stage; it is Augustanism and not classicism as a whole that he questions—and, even so, he must confess an admiration for Boileau's *Art of Poetry*. Viewed in this light, his attack on Pope has less of the air of being a pre-Wordsworthian landmark, and more of one of those periodic protests and warnings against distortion, over-refinement, affectation, and the like.

Augustanism was upheld with some reservations by Dr. Johnson (1709–84), and so, of course, was the doctrine of a selective and universalising art. He might defend " the naturalness of Shakespeare, whose dramas must not be judged by the same criteria that would be used for plays like *Cato*," but he plainly restates the old theory in the well-known passage from *Rasselas*. " The business of a poet," said Imlac, " is to examine, not the individual, but the species : to remark general properties and appearances at large : he does not number the streaks of the tulip, or describe the different shades in the verdure of the forest." The minuter discriminations must be neglected, as they are in the passage (quoted *supra*) from Waller's poem on St. James's Park. And they were still avoided in 1759, forty years before Wordsworth was to introduce a new manner of dealing with Nature [1]—the tentatives of it only, indeed, but definite enough in their direction.

Johnson did not, however, hold the Augustan doctrine entire ; while observing the Unities in *Irene*, he was led, largely by his own deep admiration for Shakespeare, to admit them to be not a *sine qua non*. Yet he remains pretty solidly a classicist ; his *London* is the Boileau-Juvenalian type of satire, his attitude to physical nature the very reverse of that self-surrender which Wordsworth should preach before the end of the century. To the question, asked by certain malcontents on the opposition benches, " whether Pope was a poet ? " he replied, " If Pope be not a poet, where is poetry to be found ? " So, evidently, a large body of poetry-readers would have replied, even as late as 1815, when Wordsworth mournfully wrote that Pope's verses " still retain their hold upon the public estimation."

[1] Cf. *The Influence of Natural Objects*, etc., written in 1799.

His practice originated, alas! the epithet "Johnsonese," and Johnsonese has come to be regarded as a kind of literary sin. It implies a heavily Latinate style, consciously balanced and portentously solemn. Granted that the flexibility of Burke is absent, and that Gibbon, with the ease of a more cynically artistic detachment, carries off successfully that which Johnson pursues and misses with such earnestness, there remains much that is solid and imposing. Take this, from *The Rambler*:

"Of those adscititious passions, some, as avarice and envy, are universally condemned; some, as friendship and curiosity, generally praised; but there are others about which the suffrages of the wise are divided, and of which it is doubted, whether they tend most to promote the happiness or increase the miseries of mankind."

It may be pompous; it is certainly noble. And more: it conveys the impression of massiveness and firmness because it is surely rooted in tradition, in the scholarship and discipline of close attention to the ancients. Which is possibly one of the reasons why Johnsonese, even if one admits it to be a late Palladian or silver age product, has that sustaining power which is lacking in the more irritant Carlylese, Browningese, Meredithese, or Kiplingese, those blessings of the Age of Wonder.

There is no reason, again, why the spectacle of Dr. Johnson keeping his head in the Highlands and refusing, nay quite unable, to yield to the spell of wild heathy mountains, should be ridiculous ; Fiona Macleod spying Dalua in every cloud-shadow is a fitter subject for mirth ; and the man who is honest enough to maintain that the porridge of the Caledonian rustic conduces to longevity no more than the turtle of city banquets deserves our admiration. With such probity sophisticated man, the centre of the classic universe, is still safe, in spite of Warton's doubts or those of Richard Hurd.[1]

One would have thought it safe enough at Exeter, where Jackson (1730–1803), going further in his admiration of Pope, defended him on occasions when Johnson boggled at his (Pope's) " improprieties." He speaks, in the comments on Pope's epitaphs, of his hope to " reinstate [this] poet in his ancient honours," and of vindicating him in spite of but with no offence to Johnson, who, however much praise he lavished, though he might at times be a little shocked, on longer works including the *Homer*, was brought up standing by the epitaphs.

Let me add that Jackson approached Gothic with caution ; it was for him too full of caprice, " dictated sometimes by good sense, more frequently by the barbarism of the times, but never by real taste, because, in the state of society in which these edifices were erected, taste did not exist." On the other hand, he revolts against the de Piles school of art ; the province of the painter,

[1] 1720–1808.

he says, is to arrange nature rather than to create. Lastly, architecture, though not to be slavishly held in Doric, Ionic, and Corinthian bonds, "will be governed by correct judgment and elegant taste."

Hurd's facing-both-ways policy has its dangers, if not for him. His *Letters on Chivalry and Romance*, in which, as Johnson said, he sets about explaining systematically, cunningly introduces the Gothic with a reassuring parallel from ancient Greece. Having gained this point and the other that Addison did not condemn the Fairy way of writing, he fustigates Hobbes, Davenant, Shaftesbury, and Rymer with a mediæval cudgel.

His view of Milton and Spenser is distorted by his Gothicism, and yet he is not wholly with the tushery faction. If the *Letters on Chivalry* had appeared in 1762, he had written, by 1766, as follows (*Idea of Universal Poetry*) : "Good sense will acknowledge no work of art but such as is composed according to the laws of its *kind*. These *kinds* . . . have yet so far their foundation in nature and the reason of things, that it will not be allowed to us to multiply or vary them at pleasure." This, and an expression, in no feeble terms, of an admiration for Aristotle, is credit for the other side, as is his editing of the *Epistle to the Pisos*; and considering his work, together with his treatment of Addison, as a whole, it would be less rash to place him among the enemies of classicism than to say that he sowed his wild oats on romantic ground, but could not finally forswear the Aristotelian cause.

Yet it is the wild oats that have won him a reputation among Victorian and Georgian critics, whose curious sense of values blinds them to the merit of his soberer work. It will not be forgotten that he stated, in the *Idea of Universal Poetry*, a theory of diction which was the exact opposite of Wordsworth's. "There should be," he wrote, " a choice of such words as are most sonorous and expressive, and such an arrangement of them as throws the discourse out of the ordinary and common phrase of conversation." This is entirely classical ; but his aberrations, Kames's impatience of rules and authority,[1] Gray's plea for a poetical sense that is not "good sense,"[2] Dyer's *Grongar Hill* mood as contrasted with that of *The Ruins of Rome*, the work of Percy and Ritson, the spurious Gothic of Walpole, Batty Langley, and Wyatt, which was succeeded by the more tiresome Gothic of Gilbert Scott, Pugin, and Bodley, go to prove that

[1] " Rude ages exhibit the triumph of authority over reason. . . . In later times, happily, reason hath obtained the ascendant ; men now assert their native privilege of thinking for themselves. . . . I am forced to except criticism, which . . . continues to be no less slavish in its principles, nor less submissive to authority, than it was originally. Bossu . . . gives many rules ; but can discover no better foundation for many of them than the practice merely of Homer and Virgil, supported by the authority of Aristotle " (*Elements of Criticism*, 1762).

[2] " . . . I insist that sense is nothing in poetry but according to the dress she wears and the scene she appears in " (Letter to the Rev. W. Mason, 1758).

increasing efforts to find room to soar meant sometimes a loss of classic orientation ; but this does not mean that classicism was moribund in the latter half of the century.

Kames also had his subversive moments ; though he admired Pope, he challenged Aristotle ; he was critically interested in Greek architecture, especially the severer styles, but found a Gothic tower beautiful according to a utility theory. He had copiously absorbed classic literature, from Homer to Perrault, and, whatever he might say in the course of his lecture, he retained the foundation of regularity, neatness, and elegance, which virtues, he noted, were fostered by the practices of gardening and architecture.

Homer, Pindar, and Horace are censured for want of connection and organic unity ; though the Aristotelian Unities, if they impede the establishment of this organic unity, are to be deprecated, and " modern critics, who for our drama pretend to establish rules founded on the practice of the Greeks, are guilty of an egregious blunder." The unity of action is, however, more desirable since " all the facts in an historical fable ought to have a mutual connection in their common relation to the grand event or catastrophe." Episodes must therefore be introduced with care, lest the unity be broken ; Homer and Virgil have successfully made such introductions, and so has the author of *Fingal*, who is brought in, *à la* Blair, cheek by jowl with the ancients.

In the matter of violence on the stage Kames is more squeamish than Sophocles :

"Ne pueros coram populo Medea trucidet,"

and heartily agrees with Addison that murder should be merely described in narrative. On the other hand, he has little good to say of Dryden and Congreve, but plenty of Shakespeare, who is "superior to all other writers in delineating passion," in "knowledge of human nature, and in unfolding even the most obscure and refined emotions." However, the examination of form must not be omitted : "His plays are defective in the mechanical part ; which is less the work of genius than experience, and is not otherwise brought to perfection but by diligently observing the errors of former compositions."

There is some sense in his notions of Beauty, Grandeur, and Sublimity. A ruin or cairn is "neutral" ; for him, at least, it has no romantic glamour, but may impress him if it is sufficiently large [1] ; an overgrown whale is not at all grand, because it has a disagreeable appearance, but " a large building, agreeable by its regularity and proportions, is grand, and yet a much larger building, destitute of regularity, has not the least tincture of grandeur." Which is severe on the classical side, since a fair modicum of asymmetry was permissible in baroque practice.

[1] Is there not something in the idea that greatness in art is to a *certain* extent a matter of quantity ?

For the two faults of sublimity, bombast, and "licentious" elevation, he goes to Dryden, Ben Jonson, and Beaumont and Fletcher. He would have found a wide field in Seneca, Garnier, Kyd, Marlowe, Shakespeare, and others; but his knowledge of Elizabethan drama was sufficiently limited for him to write that Shakespeare had no pattern, in his own or any living language, of dialogue fitted for the theatre.

On selective universality in art he is not quite "sound"—that is, he tends to quit the main position: "Every useless circumstance ought indeed to be suppressed, because every such circumstance loads the narration; but if a circumstance be necessary, however slight, it cannot be described too minutely." He thus leaves a great deal to discretion, and aggravates the perplexity about what is significant in art. In some contexts, for instance, those fatal streaks of the tulip might be found so, but seldom actually, I dare to hazard, for Kames, who is satisfied before particularities have passed the strictly economical stage of their use by Virgil, Horace, and Milton, whose "particulars" are remarkably general; by Ossian, of whom the same may be said; while in his instance from *Julius Cæsar*, the particularity is quite moderate and harmless. Of Hurd, Kames, and all such as took the more liberal and adventurous part, it might be concluded that classic foundations upheld them, and that classic capital was augmented, or squandered, by their speculations. It may be concluded of Mason, who has been represented as a secessive ; but it must be qualified. In one passage, at least, he obviously places Milton among those opposed to Romance ; it occurs in *Musæus* (1747), where Thyrsis (i.e. Milton) describes the classicising of poesy :

"... Fair poesy
Emerg'd from Gothic cloud, and faintly shot
Rekindling gleams of lustre. Her the fiend
Opprest ; forcing to utter uncouth dirge,
Runic, or Leonine."

He admits that he attempted to civilise verse, but that, in comparison with Pope (Musæus), he failed.

" I such bonds
Aim'd to destroy, hopeless that art could ease
Their thraldom, and to liberal use convert.
This wonder to achieve Musæus came."

Again, he pays Addison and his *Cato* a compliment in *Isis* (printed 1748), and Locke also, as he walks musing forth to strip " vain Falshood of her gaudy vest " ; since when—

" Alas ! how chang'd ! where now that Attic boast ?
See Gothic licence rage o'er all my coast."

In 1782 appeared his translation of Dufresnoy, which, since Dryden's time, Wills had rendered in 1754. His preface reveals something of the popularity that it had enjoyed and was still enjoying.

"Many of the precepts it contains have been so frequently repeated by later writers that they have lost the air of novelty." Nevertheless, it was in Mason's estimation worth his while to undertake a new recension. Once more the century was reminded that, at the zenith of Grecian art, " vanquish'd Nature own'd herself outdone," and warned thus :

> " Nor yet to Nature such strict homage pay
> As not to quit when genius leads the way."
> . . . . . .
> " Chuse such judicious force of shade and light
> As suits the theme, and satisfies the sight."

Elsewhere he prescribes, in portraiture, the very rules that Kent, Brown, and Shenstone applied to the garden ; rules which are intimately bound up with the selective process. When geometric banalities disgust the eye which " nauseates the tame and irksome symmetry " in unaided Nature, art must step in and correct them. Such was the aim of the contemporary gardeners, assisted by Claude and Poussin ; and it is to Claude and Poussin that Mason appeals in his *English Garden*, in which the horticulturist should feel " what Reynolds felt, when first the Vatican unbarr'd her gates." On the other hand—

> " Gothic Pomp
> Frowns and retires, his proud behests are scorn'd;
> Now Taste inspir'd by Truth exalts her voice,
> And she is heard."

The principle of the Hogarthian curve is applauded; and though Divine Simplicity cannot stomach a brazen triton in a pond, there are to be busts and urns and, " scorning a glassy penthouse of ignoble form "—

> " High on Ionic shafts he bad it tower,
> A proud rotunda; to its sides conjoin'd
> Two broad piazzas in theatric curve,
> Ending in equal porticos sublime.
> Glass roof 'd the whole, and sidelong to the south
> 'Twixt ev'ry fluted column, lightly reared
> Its wall pellucid."

At the end Simplicity is begged leave to permit him to recount the tale, not on a Gothic instrument, but a Dorian reed, which the younger generation too shall sound. But Simplicity and Skroddles [1] felt very strongly about Chinoiserie as interpreted by Sir William Chambers, not so much because Chambers held the view (which reflects Dufresnoy's teaching) that nature must be assisted by art, as that Chambers's exotic method of assistance offended him, as well as Chambers's brusque description of nature's resources, " plants, ground, and water " on which the changes are rung, " like the honest bachelor's feast, which consisted in nothing but a multiplication of his own dinner: three legs of mutton and turnips, three roasted geese, and three buttered apple pies "; hence Mason's *Heroic*

[1] So Gray spelt this nickname which Mason, in signing his letters, preferred to spell " Scroddles."

Epistle, which is nearly as good reading as the *Ode to Pinchbeck*.

For Mason and Shenstone art shaped the gay alcove, and nature painted the field; but art led nature by the nose into landscape gardens, where the "new Tivolis," cascades, spiral walks, and wriggling canals were every whit as artificial as the topiary work and geometric beds of Evelyn's day; and it was not that they were so much more natural than Chambers's pagodas as that they were different and Western. Good sense, which was often the same thing as taste, must be used in adorning England, which is not a suitable place for the exotic; Cawthorn (v. *Essay on Taste*, 1756) would banish porcelain elephants and china gods, while Taste, carrying out the selective process—

"This bids to rise, and that with grace to fall,
And bounds, unites, refines, and heightens all."

The liberalism of George Campbell's æsthetic is peculiar. He disapproved of theorists of painting, but at the remarks of de Piles, a French legislator of that art, he broke out into exclamations of dismay. De Piles's dicta betray the phase at which "imitating nature" has come to mean nothing but improving upon nature. Rubens's art, he says, is above nature, and adds paradoxically, to Campbell's vast indignation, that nature is only a copy of that great Master's works. This is the extreme statement of neo-classicism at the pole farthest away from Wordsworthian ideas on nature.

But Campbell was cantankerous and hasty ; he declares, for instance, that there is not a glimpse of meaning in the first five lines of Dryden's *Song for St. Cecilia's Day*. This depreciation of Dryden reminds one of some passages in Kames, another of the liberal school of thought.

Campbell breaks with the tradition of Universals [1] ; for him " the most vague and general " is the worst. But he has not broken away from the entire neo-classic tissue even though, like an enwebbed bluebottle, he may tug at it ; he takes over from Addison the discussion of wit, the finer kinds of which he sees and admires in Pope, while he deprecates the pun and the " clinch " as much as any of the true Augustans did ; these jokes are not used, he explains, by the person of taste—that Shaftesburian superman ; and if he is more reverent to Shakespeare than the earlier critics, he admires Congreve for his wit, and Farquhar for his humour. Nevertheless, he makes it clear that, as far north as Marischal College, the change that characterised or accompanied the late classicism was being felt.

Of other modifications not the least important was that brought about by the assault of the sentimental on the reasonable. The sentimental assaulted in France the Bastille and the nobility as well as art, but in England its onslaught was more pacific. The humanitarianism of Rousseau may have rivalled the humanism of Erasmus, or

[1] Cf. his *Philosophy of Rhetoric*, pub. 1776.

what had grown from it ; but it was Richardson who influenced both Voltaire and Rousseau. Sentimentality is, in literary politics, a bourgeois virtue, in opposition to the more aristocratic classicism. As it grew in power, it strengthened the bourgeois elements in all departments of literature, colouring the work of otherwise classical writers, notably Goldsmith. With Sterne, and to a lesser extent with Richardson, it did not preclude a sustaining cynicism ; and Sterne's tongue is seldom out of his cheek. Fielding, though he abhorred what modern slang would term Richardson's " sob-stuff," was associated with him through the common and classic basis of realising that the proper study of mankind is man and not antiquity, horrors, or history for history's, or glamour's, sake—the idols of the next phase. Fielding, as we know from his preface to *Joseph Andrews*, was well up in classic theory, and, appealing to Aristotle for support, conceives the novel (his own kind) as a comic epic poem in prose, in which nature is correctly imitated : it is as far from burlesque as Mr. Hogarth's painting is from " Caricatura."

When it comes to dealing with manners, classic imitation of nature refuses to be bound by conspiracies of silence about intimate topics ; life is to be seen steadily and whole. This is true, with all deference to Macaulay, of the Restoration Comedy. There is nothing morbid or prurient in, let us say, Defoe's *Roxana* (1724) or Fielding's *Joseph Andrews*

(1742), as there is in Lewis's *Monk* (1795) ; and Sterne's polite wit goes a long way toward preserving him from the coarseness of the smoking-room. His sense of form, the legacy of a prolonged cult of rule and authority, did much to polish that *grossièreté* which, as he observes in *The Sentimental Journey*, was not at all incompatible with the fashionable Sentimentality.[1] If Sterne's " shockingness " had been rough, boisterous, and rustic, the modern critics would never have cried out upon it as they have, while keeping discreetly silent about such things as the silly and schoolboyishly indecent dialogue which Shakespeare put into the mouths of Petruchio and Kate.

The less modified sentiment found a home in drama, being used by Sir Richard Steele as an ingredient in his palliative for the " immorality " that offended Collier. He wished to " banish out of conversation all entertainment which does not proceed from simplicity of mind, good nature, friendship and honour " ; and this was to open a convenient door for the sentimental ; *The Conscious Lovers*, which, said Parson Adams, " contains some

[1] As an instance of the ubiquity of this taste, a letter from Mason, in Germany (June 27, 1755), may be quoted : " I asked Madame Belcht if she had ever read *la petite Élogie dans la Cimetière Rustique ?* *C'est beaucoup plus jolie, je vous assure*—for I had said *fort jolie* . . . before. *Oui, Monsieur,* replied Madame Belcht, *je l'ai lue, et elle est bien jolie et mélancholique. Mais elle ne touche point le cœur, comme mes très chères Nitt Toats.*" " Nitt Toats " were the *Night Thoughts* of Young, where the melancholy variety of the sentimental might be savoured.

things almost solemn enough for a sermon," is a *locus classicus*. Young Bevil describing the preliminaries to a duel, remarks, "I abhorred the daring to offend the Author of life, and rushing into His presence—I say, by the very same act, to commit the crime against Him, and immediately to urge on His tribunal." This is strange reading in a consciously Terentian comedy; and in the reconciliation that follows there is a touch of the emasculated *comédie larmoyante* the invention of which Lanson claims for La Chaussée.[1] The hard diamond edge of Restoration comedy was thus eroded by the acid tears of sentimentality; and yet the character who was "vertueux, ou tout près de l'être," did not have it entirely his own way. There are Restoration echoes in the eighteenth century, as in the drama of Mrs. Centlivre.

The sentimental did not receive a universal and unqualified welcome; the stauncher adherents to classic wit regarded the new mode with misgivings, which, we may agree, were justified. In the *Sentimental Magasine* for April 1755 is printed an extract from *The Elements of Dramatic Criticism*,

[1] "La comédie larmoyante est un genre intermédiaire entre la comédie et la tragédie, qui s'introduit des personnages de condition privée, vertueux ou tout près de l'être, dans une action sérieuse, grave, parfois pathétique, et qui nous excite à la vertu en nous attendrissant sur ses infortunes et en nous faisant applaudir à son triomphe. La Chaussée en fut l'inventeur. (Lanson, *Nivelle de la Chaussée et la Comédie Larmoyante*.) But much of this is applicable to *The Conscious Lovers* which appeared in 1722, eleven years before La Chaussée's first dramatic effort.

by William Cooke, where the sentimental is soundly punished, called an unclassical super-session, and "a drivelling species of morality which . . . must nauseate men of sense and education. *Pamela*[1] and *The Conscious Lovers* are not spared; and this effeminate type of comedy is caustically compared with a Methodist chapel, whither a citizen may bring his wife and daughter with safety, but with no prospect of improvement. The writer cannot stomach this departure from the older comedy which (unlike the *Conscious Lovers*) is—

"The first pretence
To judgment, breeding, wit and eloquence,"

and looks upon it as something decadent.

In tragedy the classic ideal was strongly defended; there were several unfavourable elements, Elizabethan revivals and imitations (e.g. *Arden of Feversham*), the Anglo-Saxon attitudes, though even so classicised, of Mason, and the drama of Voltaire where the lachrymose element was overstressed; yet classicism was preserved in more pieces than *Cato* and *Irene*. Thomson produced craftsmanlike stuff; and though he lacked the power of Dryden, Addison, or Johnson, neither he nor *Sophonisba* is to be passed over with an "O Jemmy Thomson! Jemmy Thomson O!" on the score of occasional lapses.

[1] *Pamela*, by the way, was illustrated by Gravelot and by Joseph Highmore (1692-1780) in a purely neo-classic style.

Whitehead, a follower of Corneille, who thought that the complexity of the French intrigue would violate the unity of his subject, offered us something almost austere in his *Roman Father* (1750), whither, as into *Elfrida* and *Caractacus*, Mason's laudable offspring, the Chorus returns. Glover, constructing his *Medea* on a foundation of Seneca, recoiled from the latter's device of presenting the murder of one child on the stage, and was even more scrupulous than Euripides, as Kames was than Sophocles. But his Hecate actually appears, whereas Seneca's is reported : " ter latratus dedit et sacros edidit ignes." Elijah Fenton formed his *Mariamne*, as he declares in the epistle dedicatory, " on the model of the ancient Greek Drama."

Voltaire's tragedies, more loosely classical, were adapted by Hill and Murphy : Hoole (who makes some use of the Chorus in his *Timanthes*) may have been influenced to some extent by Voltaire before he composed *Cyrus*. Indeed, Voltaire was responsible for a fresh wave of dramatic activity in England, light upon which is thrown by Aaron Hill in his preface to *Zara* (1735). A cloud, he says, had eclipsed dramatic taste ; and he has of late been deprived of all rational pleasure from the theatre " by affectations which are grossly unnatural." Voltaire provides, in his opinion, the best basis for natural presentation ; he combines, as the prologue informs us, " a Racine's judgment with a Shakespeare's fire." The English writers, however, have lately proved themselves more undisciplined, and "warm their scenes with an ungovern'd flame." This is not being true to nature; being true to her seems to mean keeping an eye on Racine, but taking advantage of Voltaire's greater though not "ungovern'd" licence.

Voltaire, who opposed on æsthetic and private grounds the Pathetic Comedy, was nevertheless driven to resort to pathos by the demands of a fashion. As for his tragedies, they are damper with tears than is agreeable to such as are used to classic comfort. "*Ce vieillard,*" said Isménie, "*est, sans doute, un citoyen fidèle. Il pleure.*" He is a faithful citizen of the eighteenth-century stage; the sound of weeping is heard at Nineveh, in China, in Greece, in Arabia. Lachrymatory drama, whether comedy or tragedy, may imply the absence of the classic condiment wit.

Goldsmith saw and exposed this danger as far as comedy was concerned in his essay on Sentimental Comedy (1772); comedy should cause laughter, he reasonably maintains, and not tears. He and Sheridan (1751–1816) are the two peaks in the late revival of wit; but it is not the same wit, star-blasting and taking, that scorched the nibs of a Wycherley or a Swift; the sentimental and moral interregnum, the partial domestication of drama to cits' "country boxes," has done its work. Goldsmith sparkles more softly and Sheridan "bowdlerises" Vanbrugh for his *Trip to*

Scarborough. Cibber, Cumberland, and Kelly are second-rate dramatists, but their practice left its mark. The reconciliation between Lord and Lady Wronglove in Cibber's *Lady's Last Stake* (1708) and Belcour's "Sunday-school" speech that concludes Cumberland's *West Indian* (1771) are earlier and later instances of a force that Goldsmith, although he was unmistakably a revivalist of classicism, did not entirely overcome in his own work. For one thing, his personal character forbade it; he was not brazen enough to shout down these gentle but persistent voices, and, if he came to curse, he stayed to pray. Young Marlow says, "your partiality in my favour, my dear, touches me most sensibly, and were I to live for myself alone, I could easily fix my choice. But I owe too much to the opinion of a father so that—I can scarcely speak it, it affects me"; and Miss Hardcastle is enchanted at these sentiments.

CHAPTER VII
THE LATER CLASSICISM

IN Goldsmith's poetry sensibility modifies sense ; the fierce brilliance of the Augustan couplet has undergone mitigation, though the form itself is manipulated by a master of the old craft. The outlook, too, has shifted ; *The Deserted Village*, though an idealised and " selected " picture, bears traces of a stricter obedience to nature unmethodised :

> " Along thy glades, a solitary guest,
> The hollow-sounding bittern guards its nest :
> Amidst thy desert walks the lapwing flies
> And tires their echoes with unvaried cries."

" Desert walks " and " unvaried cries," however, echo backwards to Pope rather than forwards to the minuter analysis of Wordsworth who notes " the stiff lance-like shoots of pollard ash " or "birches risen in silver colonnade " (*The River Duddon*, published 1820). Cowper, on the other hand, moves onward from the sentimental (cf. *On a Goldfinch Starved to Death in his Cage*) to the romantic :

> " . . . The clouds
> That crowd away before the driving wind
> More ardent as the disk emerges more
> Resemble most some city in a blaze,
> Seen through the leafless wood."
> *The Task*, 1784.

Yet in Cowper, and in Wordsworth too, there still lingers something of the strength and majesty that classic schooling alone can impart : Cowper's handling of the couplet reflects the twilight of this nobility :

> " O blest proficiency ! Surpassing all
> That men erroneously their glory call,
> The recompense that arts or arms can yield,
> The bar, the senate, or the tented field. . . ."
> *Retirement.*

as does Wordsworth's conception of the ode :

> " Mourn, hills and groves of Attica ! and mourn
> Ilissus, bending o'er the classic urn !
> Mourn, and lament for him, whose spirit dreads
> Your once sweet memory, studious walks and shades."
> *Dion.*

If some consider it marvellous that the shepherd of the "Hebrid Isles" should have made his bow in 1748, we have the right to admire " Auster whirling to and fro, his force on Caspian foam to try " in 1820.

The technique of Augustan poetry was practised efficiently and at times almost brilliantly by Crabbe (1754–1832) ; the heroic couplet with its cæsura, combined with the proper " selective " terms, is not infrequently achieved with agreeable precision.

> " Care veils in clouds the sun's meridian beam,
> Sighs through the grove, and murmurs in the stream."

"Meridian," "sighs," "murmurs," are apt and pointed, but not unduly chromatic or particular; they satisfy our demand for what is reasonably poetic. The bed of Flora, the gin of sage Arachne, ring melodiously enough for those whose ears have not been dulled by romantic clangours. The distinction between the art of reason and that of unreason is almost as wide as that between Occidental and Oriental music; whoever is accustomed to the one will probably misunderstand the other and increase his dismay by attempting to interpret it through the system that he knows. The popular contempt for classic art is no doubt largely due to such attempts at interpretation.

At the same time Crabbe's search in his *Village* for the characteristic as opposed to the typical of Goldsmith's village tells another tale; and *The Borough* is heavily laden with that ore of minute analytic description that is such a good substitute for wit, and so helpful in eking out the later poetry and fiction. Crabbe does it excellently, having the couplet to maintain him in the equilibristic feat.

The *Lyrical Ballads* (1798) aimed a shrewd, but not fatal blow at classic orthodoxy; the book was avowedly politico-literary propaganda, setting up the language of the middle and lower classes in opposition to "the gaudiness and inane phraseology of many modern writers." Our forbears had now the chance of choosing between—

> "For thee Cassiope her chair withdraws,
> For thee the Bear retracts his shaggy paws;
> High o'er the North thy golden orb shall roll
> And blaze eternal round the wandering Pole...."
> DARWIN, *Botanic Garden*.

and—

> "By the same fire to boil their pottage
> Two poor old dames, as I have known,
> Will often live in one small cottage,
> But she, poor woman, dwelt alone."

Two sane and gifted men at least saw the dangers of the latter style; they were Jeffrey, and T. L. Peacock, who pokes not unkindly fun at "Wordsworthism" in *Melincourt*. But classic art was menaced by William (1757–1827) as well as by Goody, Blake. He was hostile to much of the theory of Reynolds, who had once told him "to work with less extravagance, and more simplicity, and correct his drawing"—a piece of advice that he would have done well to follow; and for him, as he recorded on his engraving of the Laocoön, "the outward ceremony is Antichrist."

As for the ancients, he shook his fist at them. "The Classics! it is the Classics, and not the Goths or Monks, that desolate Europe with their wars." In the agony of his obsession he cries out that Rome and Greece swept art into their maws and destroyed it, that Grecian is mathematic form while Gothic is living form. We hear the tones of revolutionary wrongheadedness; but we do not forget that Blake was apprenticed to Basire, and not uninfluenced by Flaxman, and that he had the art of generalising ; or that Wordsworth was the author of *Dion*, and strongly deprecated the excesses of the Romantic Revival, the " frantic novels, sickly and stupid German Tragedies, and deluges of idle and extravagant stories in verse."

And where does Reynolds stand ? Among the classicists, certainly, but with the left wing. He praises Vanbrugh, as we have seen, but goes so far as to hint that Vanbrugh had recourse to some of the principles of Gothic architecture. It cannot be denied that Gothic is primarily kinetic ; but to attempt for this reason to classify Baroque as a variety of Gothic is surely to go wrong.

The *Third Discourse*, one of the most, if not the most, significant, treats of selective universality in art and the grand manner, " this intellectual dignity " (he quotes) " that ennobles the painter's art." But while he approves of generalisation within the species, he does not approve of that extreme selective method " practised by some painters, who have given to Grecian heroes the airs and graces practised in the court of Lewis the Fourteenth." Excess of elegance, rhetoric and affection of this kind resulted in much that was pleasing ; but Reynolds would not permit liberties to be taken with proportion, and deprecated the " elongation of figures practised by Parmegianino " (*Tenth Discourse*). Fuseli, according to Haydon, had other and more baroque ideas concerning the grand manner: "he knew full well that he was wrong as to truth of imitation, and he kept palliating it under the excuse of 'the Grand Style.'" He said a subject should interest, astonish, or move; if it did none of these it was worth "noding by Gode." This kind of thing was happening in the days of Trafalgar; and Haydon, who laughs at Fuseli for his "grand manner" extravagance, was, some time later, taken to task by Thackeray for faults of much the same nature.[1] He tried to preserve enthusiasm for the classic by hurling acres of it at an amused or dismayed public. Payne Knight, whom he put with violence, and more than once, in the wrong, brought his eye close to Haydon's *Solomon* and said to the Prince of Wales, "distorted stuff." As regards Haydon's own work he was not far out. Haydon's art was a protest against the little manner, the particularising that can sometimes degenerate, and has in some twentieth-century as well as nineteenth-century instances, degenerated

[1] v. *A Pictorial Rhapsody*, 1840; *May Gambols*, 1844; and *Picture Gossip*, 1845. In 1786 "Peter Pindar," a lively æsthetician and follower ("copy not Nature's form too closely," he exclaims, though possibly with tongue in cheek) of Reynolds, charges West with the same obsession:

"He knoes that *bulk* is not a *jest*;
So gives us painting by the *acre*."

He is sufficiently independent to find fault with Poussin, Salvator, and the extreme baroque and anti-naturalist painters: but the fault meriting the greatest censure is violation of the *rules*.

into meanness; the protest was good but its manner unfortunately hyperbolical. Greatness in art does depend to some extent, I would once more suggest, on quantity; but to attempt to make it depend on little else but quantity, and that chiefly extensive, is a waste of much good labour.

Opie, who died two years after Trafalgar, a gentler soul than Haydon—Amelia notes his extreme placability—admired the quaint Fuseli for his classical attainments, and expressed the greatest admiration for Sir Joshua, whom he himself exceeded, as an art-theorist, in orthodoxy. Although he was praised after his death for being "no slave of system in the chains of rule," his lectures, published posthumously in 1809, show how loyally he adhered to established precept. There he tells us that the function of a master of painting is "the selection ... of what is grand, beautiful and striking in nature." He professes the fine old creed of *ut pictura poesis*, refers to the "Gothic, dry and tasteless barbarism of the old German school," and quotes Bacon in defence of a higher order of excellence than that of actual nature. He urges the view that the adjustment by art of nature's irregularities has "indeed been the general opinion of the enlightened part of mankind in all ages." Familiar with Dryden's *Parallel* and Dufresnoy, he achieves prominence as a stout apologist, in a period of rapid change, of correctness and the purest classic doctrine.

The position and genius of Jeffrey (1773-1850) emphasise the distinction between the two classic schools of thought that survived from Georgian into Victorian times. He stood for admiration of Latin culture and the relics of Augustanism; while over the way flourished the neo-Hellenists, a sect to be mentioned more fully hereafter, who partially converted more than one romantic (Keats, for example, or Shelley) and whose torch was relit subsequently by Matthew Arnold and Walter Pater.

If Jeffrey had a fault it was that of using the ferrule too forcefully; but he was not the only critic in opposition to the romantic revival who whipped with such pardonable vigour. Keats, already trounced, he flicked but lightly; but Wordsworth's *Excursion*, as we know, " will never do "—a famous utterance, justified on good grounds for those who demand wit in poetry, but leaving no room to soar, one might say. And yet Jeffrey desired originality, and assailed the *Excursion* for lack of this very quality; it had " less boldness of originality, and less even of that extreme simplicity and lowliness of tone which wavered so prettily, in the *Lyrical Ballads*, between silliness and prettiness." Elsewhere the conversation is reported to be " exceedingly dull and mystical," a good juxtaposition of epithets; good sense will be bound to find it so, and there is much to commend good sense.

Those who despise Jeffrey for praising Samuel Rogers and blaming Wordsworth, who declare that he was incapable of perceiving the subtleties of the new poetry, may ask themselves whether they are capable of perceiving the subtleties of the old, which were so clearly seen by critics of the Augustan tradition, and whether appreciation of that older poetry has not become almost a lost art. In 1819, at least, the art was not lost. Byron is less esteemed to-day than Wordsworth, in England, at least, largely because he is more able than Wordsworth to assume something of the grand manner. He admired Pope and the heroic couplet, and he was a master of that rhetoric which Peter Bells and Goody Blakes render impossible.

Jeffrey scolded Dryden for bedaubing with obscenity and transforming with rant the Shakespearean dramatic tradition, and Addison for the mawkishness of *Cato* : while the offence that he finds in Byron is heaviness with verbosity and inelegance ; in short, Byron, however much he may admire Pope, fails in practice to approach Pope's high level of elegance. Such classicism as he pretends to is imprecise and impure. Yet his literary satires show plainly enough their debt to Pope and the Horatians ; and one of his complaints in *English Bards and Scotch Reviewers* is that

" . . . Milton, Dryden, Pope, alike forgot
Resign their hallow'd bays to Walter Scott."

He cannot abide "vulgar Wordsworth," but would feel less disgusted if—

> "All our bards, more patient of delay,
> Would stop, like Pope, to polish by the way."
> *Hints from Horace.*

Unfortunately, he is himself not sufficiently patient of delay. We need but refer back to the *Essay on Criticism*, to see that Byron's "baroque" poetry is in a debased style ; and I would venture to put *Don Juan* into the category. But in this poem at least, and in some others besides the satire, he does not sacrifice the head to the heart—to transpose Coleridge's remark on the metaphysical poets ; he retains a fair savour of wit ; but with so low a standard in the craft of pointing and polishing, he cannot get rid of crudities.

In prose—and in polemic—we may find him employing the whole arsenal of extreme classicism on Pope's behalf, in the fierce little action which raged round the *Quarterly Review* between 1820 and 1825. He opposed to the naturalism of W. Lisle Bowles a theory not remote from de Piles's. Bowles, following Warton, denied Pope a place in the first rank ; further, he classed him among the poets of artifice, rather than those of nature (as understood in those Wordsworthian days). "All images," he wrote,[1] "drawn from

[1] *Reply to a Review of Spence's Anecdotes in the Quarterly Review* (1820), *Vindication of Mr. Bowles*, etc. (1821), *Final Appeal to the Literary Public Relative to Pope* (1825).

what is beautiful and sublime in the works of NATURE are more beautiful than any drawn from art. . . ." This roused Byron to assail Bowles more effectively than Gilchrist had done. In doing so, he enlarged on the extreme classic view that art transcends and improves upon nature by the selective process; that nature unhumanised is valueless—mere sand and water; and that the true landscape painter gives us not the particulars but the universals of nature. He added that the criterion of poetry was not primarily subject-matter but execution. The highest poetry was that of the most expert craftsmen—those in fact who, like Pope, were most learned in the rules and their interpretation.

But apart from these letters,[1] classic exposition lies rather in his verse than in his prose (I am thinking of the more critical of his letters), whereas with Darley the reverse is true. Mr. Abbott has done valuable work both in vindicating Darley as an art critic and showing him as one of the last of the "liberal" neo-classicists. He was one of the last, certainly, but not the least able, of the apologists for the theory of selective generalisation which Hazlitt assailed in the form that Reynolds gave to it. In the eighteen forties Darley put up a strong and laudable defence against Ruskin, who was virulently objecting to it and to Claude,

[1] Cf. *Letters on the Rev. W. L. Bowles's Strictures on Pope* (1821).

Poussin, and Salvator.[1] Darley, on the other side, was severe to Turner when on certain occasions fantasy successfully lured him from that classic highway upon which, undoubtedly, his feet had been set, as Blake's also had been; yet Darley was liberal, and had a kind word to say for the Gothic, with several gruff ones for the " Empire style " neo-classicism of David, and yet, some indignation at the neglect of Flaxman.

Yet again, it will help us to take his bearings if we remember that he got into a rage with Johnson for his *Lives*, and drove Serjeant Talfourd, the author of neo-Hellenist tragedies, such as were *Ion* and *The Athenian Captive*, almost to desperation, by his criticism of the former play. In one letter he prophesies that Talfourd will produce " Euripides put into curl," and he does; or rather, keeping an eye on the marble of Landor, I would say that he produced agreeable stucco like the old quadrant of Regent Street, very Anglo-Greek,

[1] Somewhat earlier in the century Polwhele was declaiming to his audiences at Truro heroic couplets calculated to promote a good taste that includes familiarity with Claude and Salvator:

" Salvator flings
His random foliage o'er the murky stream,
And trembles through the leaves a fitful gleam!
. . . . .
Shall crystal riv'let, shall a roseate bloom
From pleasant Claude, relieve the sullen gloom ? "

Polwhele profited by the study of Burke on the sublime and beautiful, and Shaftesbury's theory of moral-æsthetic taste, which, he points out, is Platonic.

but by no means undignified, as anyone who buys a Talfourd at the sixpenny bookstall and reads him, will be agreeably surprised to find.

But Darley has other ideas of grandeur; he may countenance universals, but not *Ion*, and not Regent Street, which he calls "a gigantic display of littleness." Stucco, no less than marble, has its beauties; but if littleness, which was certainly gaining ground at this time, was evident in the Quadrant, it was not lacking in some of Darley's own verse—Dwerga always seems to me an incarnation of one aspect of littleness. But there were traces of a careless and not unclassic grandeur in Byron; there were the marks of the grand manner in Landor's marble and classic prose, side by side with the romantic testiness.

Landor was a scholar, but not a very deep one; he knew and loved, though rather capriciously, his Latin and Greek poets. Further, at a time when the gates were opening to the wayward, emotive sort of criticism, he demanded, if he did not always achieve, care and method.

In the *Pentameron* we find him opposed to the excess of fantasy that is Gothic whatever else it may be; "none of the imitative arts should repose on writings and distortions. Tragedy herself, unless she lead from Terror to Pity, has lost her way." This sounds very Aristotelian and correct; and in the *Imaginary Conversations* he presents Aristotle legislating for the poetic of this world, while the nebulous Plato descends from Cloud-cuckoo Land to kick the poets through the streets. But in the " Chatham and Chesterfield," after he has blamed Plato's attitude towards the poets, and also " the apes who chatter as they pick out the scurf of Shakespeare," he holds up Shakespeare as the great proof that there is a poetic truth which appeals to the passions, apart from rational truth.

Landor's prose is clearer and harder than Talfourd's blank verse; yet the matter of the prose is often confusing to those who look for vestiges of a tendency or school, because he is, at first sight, curiously untypical of either classic or romantic. The " period interest " of his conversations is certainly the latter; and he himself was, I take it, a romantic who wished to classicise himself. In the style there are some traces of restlessness which set it at a distance from those of the Augustan and earlier Georgian masters. It often derives from the tradition, but it cannot strictly be said to be of it. There is not space to set passages here for comparison, but a brief examination of Addison, Johnson, and Landor will suffice to indicate how far the last has managed to stray down his less level by-way. And as long as we recollect that with people like Campbell and Kames there had been already some impatience of legal order, some wavering between the reason and unreason of art, we shall not feel it so puzzling to find the same man writing of—

"... Poussin's nymph-frequented woods,
  His templed heights and long-drawn solitudes,"
and—

"... One warm sunset of Ausonian Claude,"

or declaring that the Greek Muses were sedate, never obstreperous ; and yet perpetrating in *The Citation and Examination of William Shakespeare* (tilley valley, 'tis woundily dull !) as arrant and obstreperous a piece of tushery as was ever sold in a Rye curio shop. The Epistle to Bailey on " the Classick and Romantick " provides a further instance of his deliberately (or not) perverse blindness to fundamental differences. What can we say of this—

" Goldsmith was classical, and Gray almost ;
  So was poor Collins, heart-bound to Romance ? "

No doubt that it has the truth in it ; but the next line of the poem, " Shelley and Keats, those southern stars, shone higher," baffles us, and suggests that Landor's critic muse was too often floundering in the dark, unbeaconed by even the flair of the connoisseur.

His lively interest in the Greeks and his attempt to impart a Greek atmosphere to some of the Conversations may reflect some of the neo-Hellenism that was now, meteorically, " in the air " ; but he is not thus constituted a pillar of the neo-Hellenistic cause, which by this time was almost elderly. The publication in mid-eighteenth century of such works as Dawkins and Wood's *Illustrations of Palmyra and Baalbec* (1750), Adam's *Spalatro* (1760), and Stuart's *Athens* (1762), gave an impetus to the new taste which during the first decades of the next century was to bear much architectural fruit. Indeed, Soane's *Bank of England* bears an earlier date—1788. The somewhat notorious St. Pancras Church was begun in 1819, three years after the publication of Wilkins's *Atheniensia*.[1]

Poor Collins may have been heart-bound to romance: but he is certainly to be numbered, like Glover, among the early Greek revivalists. The taste is reflected, through the glass of his own classical preferences, in some of the Odes, such as those to Liberty, Fear, and Simplicity: and Glover reflects it with more power but less charm in his *Leonidas* (1737), *Medea* (1761), and *Athenaid* (published 1787, two years after his death). These are sumptuous monuments of classic industry: yet some of us may prefer *Admiral Hosier's Ghost*. Leonidas alone provides a fortune in rhetoric, colour, and picture. Meliboeus occupies among his goats a Salvatorian scene, and Artemisia disembarks between an avenue of sailors, while a golden ray shoots from her standard. There are a thousand further delights, Homeric, sublime, or beautiful: and a length fatal or alluring according to taste and diligence. The poet laureate accuses,

[1] Other works of this revival were Leake's *Researches* (1814) and Dodwell's *Classical Tour* (1819).

in his essay on Keats, these older generations of having misunderstood Greek art. This might be debated at length : but the interest in that art and legend displayed by poets, dilettanti, sculptors, architects, and artists—of whom James Barry (1741–1806), of *The Victors of Olympus*, is a noteworthy instance, cannot be questioned.

The Elgin marbles, which arrived in 1803, and exacerbated the not cordial relations of Haydon and Knight, furthered the later interest in Greek art : but impetus had already been given to the movement not only by the published books aforesaid, but by the appearance in England of the Portland Vase, which was purchased by Sir William Hamilton from the Barberini family in 1770. Erasmus Darwin, a friend of Wedgwood's, bidding—

". . . Mortality rejoice and mourn
O'er the fine forms of Portland's mystic urn,"

wrote a long descriptive note on it in *The Economy of Vegetation*. Wedgwood, who also profited by the antiques that Sir William had dug up at Herculaneum, multiplied copies of the " mystic urn " : but he was already a classicist with Greek leanings, associated with others of a cognate taste, like John Bacon the sculptor, who modelled for him an Apollo and Daphne, and won the first gold medal for sculpture in the Royal Academy (1769) with his Æneas bearing Anchises ; or John Flaxman, whom Mr. Matthew discovered as a little boy seated behind a counter reading Cornelius Nepos. It was Matthew who introduced Flaxman to Homer.

Wedgwood, with something of an Etruscan bias, delighted in the Grecian manner, in which taste he was assisted by the painter Wright of Derby, who drew for him such pictures as "The Corinthian Maid or Penelope Unravelling Her Web"; while Mrs. Landre modelled tritons, naiads, and sphinxes. He himself was far from imitating his ancient models with complacent acquiescence; a Wedgwood vase, or a Flaxman design, for that matter, is classic, original, and English, just as in its way the work of Wren had been.

Here was a formidable rival to the neo-Gothic: we find Stothard, himself a follower of Sir Joshua and Rubens, if one may judge by his style of painting, hesitating enough to praise Gothic, but preferring the Greek. And the "Grecian Gusto" has increased in strength since his day and those of Athenian Stuart, Revett, and the Dilettanti Society. After St. Pancras the Ionic British Museum was begun in 1823; Cockerell, the designer of the Taylorian Building at Oxford (1841–2), shuddered at Gothic; and Sir E. M. Barry (d. 1880), though his mention here may be questioned since at heart he was no classic purist, but an architect of the neo-Baroque, declared the Gothic taste to be no more than a passing fashion, which was a shrewd guess at truth. Modern London affords copious evidence of this: and even amidst such a mediævalising movement as that of the Pre-Raphaelites we may observe Woolner paying an Homeric compliment to Gladstone, and the ungothic subject of his Virgilia mourning the banishment of Coriolanus.

A friend of Athenian Stuart's who gave evidence together with Flaxman on behalf of the genuineness of the Elgin Marbles was Joseph Nollekens (1735-1823) the sculptor, who supported not too intellectually (he is said never to have read Homer) the classical taste. He had travelled in Italy: and Rowlandson has caricatured him modelling a Venus, perhaps from the charming Miss Coleman, who is seated among a pantheon nearly as unclad as herself. Somewhat uncompromisingly, he set man in the centre of the world of artistic representation, and had no feeling for the beauty of vegetable nature; more than Flaxman, or, as his biographer comments, than the Greeks and Romans themselves, he adhered exclusively to the human form. He admired Poussin, prints of whose paintings he collected; and Smith suggests that his own sculpture was not uninfluenced by the figures of that master, especially in his rendering of drapery.

The fresh spate of Hellenism proved invigorating to some of the new "emotive" poets, as the marble-edged canals of the Augustans did not. If it stimulated a Porson to scholarship and a Smirke to lay heavy loads on Bloomsbury earth, it inspired the aeromantics of Shelley and Keats in a certain measure. But these two, when they make use of Greek material, remain clothers of their own romanticism in the chiton and the peplum; they are not primarily classicists, while Peacock is. The whole difference and distance between the two positions may be seen in Peacock's *Four Ages of Poetry* and Shelley's *Defence*. Peacock laughed at the gentleman who held that " all that is artificial is anti-poetical "; he laughed at Scott, Byron, Southey, Wordsworth, and Coleridge. He might be heard epigrammatising on the new poetic fashions: " these disjointed relics of tradition and fragments of second-hand observation being . . . conducted on what Mr. Coleridge calls a new principle (that is, no principle at all), compose a modern antique compound of frippery and barbarism, in which the puling sentimentality of the present time is grafted on the misrepresented ruggedness of the past. . . ."

This essay, ruthless, reasoned, and many-edged with the wit of the satirical rogue, serves well as an antidote to certain ineffectual wing-flappings in Shelley's *Defence* : the two different idioms are as of two different worlds—that, if you will, of reality, and that of fantasy. " Poetry . . . makes immortal" (we dive out of reality) " all that is best and most beautiful in the world. . . . It transmutes all that it touches, and every form moving within the radiance of its presence is changed by wondrous sympathy to an incarnation of the spirit which it breathes: its sweet alchemy turns to gold the poisonous waters which flow from death through life." And so, starting from what is nothing more or less than the familiar selective theory, we pass on to the magical theory of poetry. From selection by man we arrive at the transmutation not only of "what is best and most beautiful," but even of "the poisonous waters" by that alchemic thing poetry.

Shelley was affected by the Greek as by other "sources": and it would be as well to remember that these poets of the infancy of the revolt from reason were still too near to it to be as completely detached from its tradition as they aspired to be. It is not merely a passage or so in the *Defence* that suggests this: Shelley, had he ballasted himself and put forth manfully from the haven of *Peter Bell the Third* might have—dare one breathe it?—risen to the mordant peaks of satire. There was promise in *Peter Bell the Third*, but, alas!

> "What does the rascal mourn or hope,
>   No longer imitating Pope,
>   In that Barbarian Shakespeare poking?"

The further from Pope, the wider are floodgates opened to the tide of all that can excite the pens of cosmically disposed sciolists and mystagogues. Keats, too, was affected by the Greek, and by good things other than it; by Milton, Latin mythology, or Claude's *Enchanted Castle*. His Hellenism is touched upon by Landor in the *Conversations*:

"when it was a matter of wonder how Keats, who was ignorant of Greek, could have written his Hyperion, Shelley . . . gave as a reason 'because he was a Greek.'" De Quincey pulls this obvious flimsiness to pieces, but misses the idea of an Anglo-Greek infection by this time endemic, if no more. It has during the nineteenth century modified the essentially romantic art of that period much as Renaissance classicism modified Shakespeare, allowing, of course, for the necessary differences in the feeling for Antique.

While it survived through being put to such use, Augustanism languished like a deserted bogle: and in 1848 De Quincey attempted to extinguish at a blow Pope, Augustanism, the didactic poem, and Lucretius, passing in conclusion this ominous sentence: "it is no longer advisable to reprint the whole of either Dryden or Pope." That we are more sensible to-day is proved by the recent revival of interest in Pope and Dryden, whom De Quincey failed to quell. And even in his day the ambrosial coterie of *Maga* had something to say for "Pop." As for "imitating Pope," it is curious hearing that the heroic couplet was revived by winners and competitors for the Newdigate prize at Oxford during the nineteenth century: and this, too (as the President of Magdalen has assured me), without any official stipulation that the couplet was required.

On the other hand, it seems strange at first that

one of the late inheritors of Augustan form, Lord Macaulay, should also have been ranked against Pope : Addison he admired, it is true, but he lacked in general the *flair* for literary criticism. It is his style and his love of order that link him to the classic tradition, that render him attractive to Taine and Legouis, the latter of whom notes that his equilibrated and architectural quality is without doubt of a French type, adding that "*pour lui la vérité est avant tout dans l'ordre*." For carrying over that ordered, architectural brilliance from the age of Gibbon into that of Victoria, for this alone he becomes worthy of the classic laurel ; and you might add, for very little else. But the frontier of our province is already crossed in historical pursuit, and we find the twilight of the gods upon us.

It has been noticed how English classicism at all its varying phases has retained English characteristics : and how it has proved to be much more elastic than its detractors would have us believe.

We have seen that poetry, being, as Arnold quotes once more in 1880, "φιλοσοφώτερον καὶ σπουδαιότερον," and dealing in generalities rather than in those particulars that are the business of the historian, acquires the right, shared by graphic art, to rearrange and even to recreate nature, which is therefore subservient to man, creator, and artist : that rules are evolved from tradition for this difficult and responsible task ; and that the ideal set is the type, in preference to the character. Correctness and good sense, grandeur and dignity, have been the aims : and the sublime and grand manners have admitted a not unreasonable use of the kinetic element, a regulated but not unduly restricted art. Classicism does not cease to be itself because it develops, and to claim that all the changes and modifications which occurred from Pope's time onward were warnings or beginnings of the romantic revival would seem to be almost absurdly rash. Grandeur, which implies space, and rule, which implies discipline, have a tonic and sustaining effect even on the inferior artist : and we may demand a hearing for the plea not only that the worst classic art is better than the worst romantic, but that there is an average higher level of craftsmanship, and even a greater amount of work that does not offend and disgust, among the classics. Let us consider Stephen Duck on Richmond Park (1731), where he follows rather lamely the descriptive way of Denham and Pope. But as a Claudesque effort it might be much more banal : and there are grateful passages in *The Journey to Marlborough*, etc., where the baroque *décor* of purple shells, curling vines (a favourite padding, or, one might say, stuffing, of Duck's), and abstract ladies refreshes us. But there is also more than one example of the lowest common multiple of Augustan cliché :

> " There fair Pomona loads the blushing Boughs ;
> See, fruitful Ceres crowns the Vales with Corn,
> And fleecy Flocks the verdant Hills adorn."

The technique is that of a mechanical tessellation, but the pseudo-Roman pavement so made is firm to stand on : it will not let us down ; whereas, in the age of wonder every footstep is jeopardised. If Shelley touches the highest, he sinks all the deeper below water-level : and we may flounder dismally in marishes where his characteristic froth bears the semblance of dry land.

> " Then weave the web of the mystic measure ;
> From the depths of the sky and the ends of the earth,
> Come, swift spirits of might and pleasure,
> Fill the dance and the music of mirth."

We leave him but to find more treacherous because seemingly safer going as, further on, we approach the *Angel in the House*.

> " Our confidences heavenwards grew
> Like foxglove buds, in pairs disclosed."

Pomona aid us ! There may be glories of indiscipline, but can they outweigh its shames ? At least there remains to the dreariest moments of a disciplined age something more than mere atony. As for the glories, let us admire them without an optic glass, and cease to argue that because our favourite poet (Swinburne, or Francis Thompson) wrote great poetry, therefore neither Pope, nor Pomfret, nor Parnell wrote poetry at all.

INDEX OF PRINCIPAL NAMES

Addison, 65, 66, 76–82, 97, 100, 109 n., 116, 119, 121, 125, 141, 146, 155
Aristotle, 12, 32, 34, 39, 45, 57, 60, 65, 73, 75, 82, 87, 100, 104, 116, 117 n., 118, 126, 145
Ascham, 12–15, 18, 32

Bacon (F.), 37–41, 42, 49, 50, 72
Barclay, 8, 24
Barry, Sir E. M., 150
Beaumont, 120
Bellori, 54, 55, 65
Blackmore, 59, 85, 87–9, 91, 102
Blair, 99–102, 118
Blake, 71, 105, 136–7, 144
Boileau, 58, 59, 65, 73, 78, 82, 85, 91–3, 98, 100, 108, 110, 111, 112, 113
Bosanquet, 31, 39, 46
Bossu, le, 77, 92, 111, 117 n.
Bowles, 142, 143
Buckingham, 79, 89, 110
Burke, 99, 101, 103, 114, 144 n.
Byron, 141–3, 145, 152

Campbell, 124–5, 146
Chambray (see Fréart).

Chaussée, la, 110, 138
Cheke, 14, 17
Claude, 46, 61, 83, 96, 98, 108, 122, 143, 144 n., 147, 153
Coleridge, 48, 49, 142, 152
Collins, 105, 147, 148
Corneille, 31, 68, 75, 98, 130
Cowley, 30, 49–51, 59, 76, 100, 110
Cowper, 51, 133–4
Crabbe, 134–5

Daniel, 20, 21
Darley, 46, 143–5
Darwin, E., 89, 93, 94, 136, 149
Davenant, 40, 42, 45, 49, 52–4, 116
Denham, 30, 47–8, 51, 80, 93, 110, 156
Dryden, 9, 21, 29, 31, 33, 39, 46, 51, 54, 58, 59, 62, 63, 67–75, 76, 79, 80, 81, 92, 97, 99, 100, 101, 110, 119, 120, 121, 125, 129, 139, 141, 154
Dufresnoy, 46, 55, 62, 65, 96, 103, 104, 121, 123, 139

Erasmus, 7, 8, 17, 21, 83, 112, 125

INDEX OF PRINCIPAL NAMES

Flaxman, 137, 144, 149–51
Fréart, 65, 66, 85, 87
Fuseli, 99, 137, 138, 139

Garnier, 25, 27, 28, 120
Gascoigne, 10, 23, 25, 26
Gerard, 103, 104
Gildon, 59, 79, 84
Goldsmith, 45, 126, 131–3, 135, 147
Gray, 105, 111, 117, 123 *n.*, 147

Harris, 94–7, 111
Harvey, 13, 14, 19, 20, 34
Haydon, 96, 137–9, 149
Hobbes, 41, 43, 44, 49, 55, 57, 58, 61, 72, 75, 89, 90, 91, 92, 116
Hogarth, 87, 102, 103, 104–7, 126
Homer, 14, 19, 22, 80, 83, 91, 100, 103, 107, 109, 112, 117, 118, 150, 151
Horace, 12, 14, 22, 28, 31, 32, 34, 35, 43, 45, 59, 65, 67, 73, 82, 92, 93, 96, 97, 109, 110, 111, 118, 120, 142
Hulme, 29, 31, 52, 101
Hurd, 115, 116, 120

Jeffrey, 136, 140, 141
Johnson, Dr., 112–15, 116, 129, 144, 146
Jones, I., 40, 65, 66, 71
Jonson, Ben, 26, 31, 33–6, 72, 74, 120

Kaimes (Kames), 31, 84, 85, 117, 118–20, 130, 146

Keats, 140, 147, 149, 151, 153, 154
Knight, 107, 138, 149
Kyd, 17, 27, 28, 120

Landor, 144, 145–7, 153
Langbaine, 74–5
Lessing, 31, 64
Locke, 76, 77, 78, 85, 91, 121
Longinus, 73, 79 *n.*, 100, 101, 102, 107, 109 *n.*, 111
Lyle, 15, 16, 19, 23

Macaulay, 126, 155
Mason, 46, 63 *n.*, 117, 121–4, 127 *n.*, 129, 130
Milton, 10, 25, 46, 47, 79, 80, 92, 93, 96, 99, 100, 101, 103, 105, 109, 110, 116, 120, 121, 153

Nashe, 11, 13, 17–19, 24
Nollekens, 151

Opie, 139

Palladio, 64, 65, 66, 87, 91
Peacock, 136, 152
Perrault, 59, 60, 67, 118
Piles, de, 115, 124, 142
Plautus, 22, 26, 74
Pope, 22, 25, 30, 38, 46, 50, 52, 58, 75, 79, 80, 81, 82–4, 86, 87, 88, 97, 109, 110, 111, 112, 113, 115, 118, 121, 125, 133, 141, 142, 143, 153, 154, 155, 156, 157
Poussin, 46, 60, 61, 82, 96, 98, 122, 138, 144, 147, 151

INDEX OF PRINCIPAL NAMES

Prior, 84, 85, 97, 110
Purcell, 63, 69, 70, 72

Rapin, 38, 45, 73, 75, 83
Reynolds, 46, 63, 122, 136, 137, 138 n., 139, 143, 150
Rubens, 51, 64, 72, 104, 124, 150
Ruskin, 36, 54, 62, 98, 112, 143
Rymer, 56, 58, 116

Salvator, 31, 96, 99, 105, 111, 135 n., 144
Seneca, 15, 16, 21, 23, 26, 27, 120, 130
Shaftesbury, 31, 85–8, 91, 92, 95, 97, 116, 144 n.
Shakespeare, 8, 15, 16, 17, 26, 27, 28–31, 57, 74, 75, 81, 83, 101, 102, 109, 110, 112, 113, 119, 120, 125, 127, 130, 146, 147, 153, 154
Shelley, 82, 83, 94, 140, 147, 151, 152, 153, 154, 157
Sidney, 12, 19, 23, 24, 31, 32–4, 37, 55, 74, 92

Spenser, 10, 13, 20, 24, 34, 35, 47, 49, 92, 93, 97, 109, 110, 116
Swift, 59, 60, 63, 88, 99, 109, 110, 131

Tatius, Achilles, 22, 23, 24, 80
Thomson, 64, 97, 98, 111, 129
Thornhill, 51, 62, 63, 64

Vanbrugh, 31, 63, 64, 65, 67, 76, 108, 131, 137
Virgil, 11, 17, 18, 22, 24, 80, 91, 97, 100, 103, 109, 111, 117 n., 118, 120
Voltaire, 57, 110, 126, 129, 130, 131

Waller, 31, 51, 100, 110, 113
Warton, J., 84, 97, 106, 109–11, 115, 142
Wedgwood, 169, 170
Wordsworth, 91, 96, 113, 117, 133, 134, 137, 139, 140, 141, 152
Wren, 63, 65, 67, 87, 150

Young, 109, 111, 137